Texas Business Torts Litigation Handbook

Haynes and Boone, LLP

The material contained herein represents the opinions of the authors and editors. Nothing contained in this book is to be considered as the rendering of legal advice for specific cases, and readers are responsible for otaining such advise from their own legal counsel. This book is intended for educational and informational purposes only.

ISBN: 0-9789073-0-2

Library of Congress Control Number:

Discounts are available for books ordered in bulk. Requests for information should be addressed to:

Haynes and Boone
901 Main, Suite 3100
Dallas,Texas 75202
www.haynesboone.com

Printed in the United States of America.

CONTENTS

CONTENTS

v

III. CIVIL CONSPIRACY 35

IV. DEFAMATION OF A BUSINESS ENTITY AND BUSINESS DISPARAGEMENT 45

V. FRAUD

VI. MISAPPROPRIATION OF TRADE SECRETS AND IMPROPER USE OF CONFIDENTIAL INFORMATION   78

ACKNOWLEDGMENT

Haynes and Boone, LLP and the Business Litigation Section extend special thanks to its attorneys who contributed their ·time, effort and skill in writing and editing this book, including: Rick Anigian, Jason Augustine, Todd Baker, Ted Baroody, Spencer Bartlett, Courtney Biery, George Bramblett, Marty Brimmage, Chip Brooker, Altresha Burchett, Charles Cantu, Deborah Coldwell, David Drez, Russ Emerson, Earl Harcrow, David Harper, Michael Hood, Patrick Keating, Patrick Kelly, Tom Kurth, Pete Marketos, Debbie McComas, Ryan McComber, Aimee Minick, Dixie Newnam, Travis Perry, Phillip Philbin, Don Templin, Victor Vital, and Tom Williams.

If you would like further information regarding any of the topics discussed in this handbook, please contact Rick Anigian at 214.651.5633, rick.anigian@haynesboone. com.

Disclaimer

The views of the authors are theirs alone and do not represent those of Haynes and Boone, LLP or its clients. The book is intended to assist the reader in identifying issues and formulating strategy, and not as legal advice. No substitute exists for meticulously reexamining the rules and laws in every situation or consulting a lawyer, however, and the authors and Haynes and Boone, LLP make no warranty herein, and disclaim all implied warranties.

INTRODUCTION

This book is designed to guide both attorneys and business people through the types of claims and defenses most commonly raised in business disputes.

Organized by cause of action, each section outlines the elements of each cause of action as recognized by Texas courts, the general rules, major exceptions, required proof, the remedies or damages, and common defenses generally applicable to each. We have not provided an exhaustive discussion of any of the claims or defenses but intend for this handbook to serve as a quick reference guide. The book includes descriptions for each of the following areas: Aiding and Abetting; Breach of Fiduciary Duty; Business Disparagement; Civil Conspiracy; Defamation of a Business Entity; Fraud; Misappropriation of Trade Secrets; Negligent Misrepresentation; Tortious Interference with Contractual or Business Relations; and Unfair Competition.

We believe that you will find this handbook to be valuable and reliable.

I. AIDING AND ABETTING

A. Introduction

B. Assisting or Encouraging

    (1) Elements

        (a) Primary Actor's Breach of Duty

        (b) Defendant's Knowledge

        (c) Defendant's Intent

        (d) Defendant's Substantial Assistance or Encouragement

    (2) Examples

C. Assisting and Participating

    (1) Elements

        (a) Primary Actor's Tort

        (b) Substantial Assistance

        (c) Defendant's Participation in the Tort

    (2) Examples

D. Concert of Action

    (1) Elements

        (a) The Commission of an Intentional Tort

        (b) A Highly Dangerous Tort

        (c) The Defendant's Agreement

A. Introduction

Aiding and abetting involves the imposition of joint liability on a defendant for a plaintiff's injury that is caused by a third party. Restatement (Second) of Torts § 876. Texas courts have long recognized aiding and abetting liability when the defendant knowingly participates in a third-party fiduciary's breach of duty to the plaintiff. See *Kinzbach Tool Co. v. Corbett-Wallace Corp.*, 160 S.W.2d 509, 514 (Tex. 1942); *Hendricks v. Thornton*, 973 S.W.2d 348, 372 (Tex. App.—Beaumont 1998, pet. denied).

To "aid" means to assist, and to "abet" means to encourage, advise, or instigate. Black's Law Dictionary 76 (8th ed. 2004). In the current caselaw, as well as in the Restatement (Second) of Torts, the words "assisting" and "encouraging" are often substituted for the traditional language of "aiding" and "abetting."

There are three theories under which a defendant may be held liable for a third party's actions under the umbrella of "aiding and abetting": (1) assisting and encouraging; (2) assisting and participating; and (3) concert of action. See Restatement (Second) of Torts § 876. These theories require different levels of knowledge, intent, participation, and culpable conduct on the part of the defendant.

The Texas Securities Act also provides for a statutory aiding and abetting cause of action. Tex. Rev. Civ. Stat. art. 581-33F(2) (Vernon Supp. 2005).

B. Assisting or Encouraging

A defendant is liable for "assisting or encouraging" the primary actor's tort if the defendant knows that the primary actor's conduct constitutes a breach of duty and gives the primary actor substantial assistance or encouragement. Restatement (Second) of Torts § 876(b). This is what is traditionally thought of as civil "aiding and abetting." The Texas Supreme Court has not had reason to specifically adopt the Restatement of Torts' definition of assisting or encouraging, but has noted that most jurisdictions have adopted this particular formulation of the tort and indicated that it would likely follow suit. *Juhl v. Arrington*, 936 S.W.2d 640, 644 (Tex. 1996).

(1) Elements

The essential elements of a cause of action for assisting or encouraging are:

(1) the primary actor's breach of duty;
(2) the defendant's knowledge;
(3) the defendant's intent; and
(4) the defendant's assistance or encouragement.

Juhl, 936 S.W.2d at 644; *Shinn v. Allen*, 984 S.W.2d 308, 311 (Tex. App.—Houston [1st Dist.] 1998, no pet.); *Stein v. Meachum*, 748 S.W.2d 516, 518-19 Tex. App.—Dallas 1988, no writ); *Crisp v. Southwest Bancshares Leasing Co.*, 586 S.W.2d 610, 613 (Tex. App.—Amarillo 1979, writ ref'd n.r.e.); Restatement (Second) of Torts § 876(b).

(a) Primary Actor's Breach of Duty

A claim for assistance or encouragement of a tort requires the primary actor to have committed a tort in the first place. See *Crisp*, 586 S.W.2d at 613. In order to prove that the defendant has assisted or encouraged the primary actor's tort, the plaintiff first must prove that the primary actor's actions constitute a tort. To do so, the plaintiff must show: (1) that the primary actor owed a duty to the plaintiff; and (2) that the primary actor breached this duty. *Kline v. O'Quinn*, 874 S.W.2d 776, 786 (Tex. App.—Houston [14th Dist.] 1994, writ denied).

Where the alleged primary tort is breach of a fiduciary duty, the plaintiff will need to show the existence of a fiduciary relationship. *Id.* Such a relationship exists when the primary actor is under a duty to act or give advice for the benefit of another upon matters within the scope of the relation. *Id.* Not every business relationship results in the creation of a fiduciary duty. One party's subjective trust of another does not alone indicate that confidence is placed in another in the sense demanded by fiduciary relationships. *Id.* The fact that one party trusts another and relies upon the other's promise to perform a contract does not rise to a confidential relationship. *Crim Truck & Tractor Co. v. Navistar Int'l Transp. Corp.*, 823 S.W.2d 591, 594-95 (Tex. 1992).

(b) Defendant's Knowledge

A claim for assistance or encouragement requires that the defendant have knowledge that the primary actor's conduct constitutes a tort. See *Juhl*, 936 S.W.2d at 644. If the plaintiff cannot prove that the defendant knew that the primary actor was breaching his or her duty, the defendant cannot be held liable under the assistance or encouragement theory. Restatement (Second) of Torts § 876(b).

(c) Defendant's Intent

A claim for assistance or encouragement requires that the defendant have the intent to assist the primary actor in committing the tort. According to the Texas Supreme Court, the plaintiff is required to show "an unlawful intent, i.e., knowledge that the other party is breaching a duty and the intent to assist that party's actions." *Juhl*, 936 S.W.2d at 644 (quoting *Payton v. Abbott Labs*, 512 F. Supp. 1031, 1035 (D. Mass. 1981)). It is not necessary to demonstrate the presence of an actual agreement between the defendant and the primary actor. *Id.*

(d) Defendant's Substantial Assistance or Encouragement

A claim for assistance or encouragement requires that the defendant give the primary actor assistance or encouragement. Anyone who "commands, directs, advises, encourages, procures, instigates, promotes, controls, aids, or abets a wrongful act by another, has been regarded as being as responsible as the one who commits the acts." *Francis v. Kane*, 246 S.W.2d 279, 281 (Tex.Civ.App.—Amarillo 1951, no writ) (quoting S2 Am. Jur 454, p 114). Furthermore, this assistance or encouragement must be regarded as "substantial."

Where one person assists another in committing a tort, both are principals and liable in damages for any injury inflicted. *Stein*, 748 S.W.2d at 518 (Tex. App.—Dallas 1988, no writ). The defendant's encouragement of the primary actor to commit the tort is also sufficient to allow for a finding of the defendant's joint liability.

In order to prevail, the plaintiff must prove that the assistance or encouragement given to the primary actor was a substantial factor in causing the tort. Restatement (Second) of Torts § 876(b) cmt. d. It is possible that a party's assistance or encouragement of the primary actor's tortious actions may be so slight as to not result in liability. *Id.* In determining whether the assistance or encouragement is a *substantial* factor in causing the tort, the court looks at five factors: (1) the nature of the act encouraged; (2) the amount of assistance given by the defendant; (3) the defendant's presence or absence at the time of the tort; (4) the defendant's relation to the primary actor; and (5) the defendant's state of mind. *Id*; *Juhl*, 936 S.W.2d at 644. Even if the defendant's assistance or encouragement were a substantial factor in causing the tort, the defendant will not be held liable for those acts committed by the primary actor that were not foreseeable by the defendant. Restatement (Second) of Torts § 876(b) cmt. d.

(2) Examples

(1) In *Kline*, 874 S.W.2d 776, the court held that joint liability for breach of fiduciary duty could attach to the defendant, a bank, where the bank was a creditor of the primary actor and was alleged to have knowingly and actively participated in the breach of fiduciary duty. Because no fiduciary relationship was established between the plaintiff and the primary actor, the claim failed.

(2) In *Forum Fin. Group v. President & Fellows of Harvard Coll.*, 173 F.Supp.2d 72, 97-99 (D. Maine 2001), the court found the defendant, the agent of the college, jointly liable for fraudulent misrepresentation, negligent misrepresentation, and tortious interference with prospective economic advantage. The defendant directed and supervised those who misrepresented the plaintiff's prospective profits and interfered with the prospective economic advantage.

C. Assisting and Participating

The tort of "assisting and participating," as it is defined by the Restatement (Second) of Torts, has not been adopted by the Texas Supreme Court. The

Court has, however, long recognized the defendant's participation in the tortious act of the primary actor as sufficient to impose liability on the defendant. See *City of Fort Worth v. Pippen*, 439 S.W.2d 660, 665 (Tex. 1969); *Kinzbach Tool Co.*, 160 S.W.2d at 514, ("where a third party knowingly participates in the breach of duty of a fiduciary, such third party becomes a joint tort-feasor with the fiduciary and is liable as such.")

Unlike "assisting or encouraging" a tort, the Restatement's conception of "assisting and participating" does not require knowledge that the action constitutes a tort. Restatement (Second) of Torts § 876 (c) cmt. e. However "assisting and participating" does require that the defendant's actions by themselves constitute the breach of a duty that the defendant and primary actor jointly owe the plaintiff. *Id.*

(1) Elements

As described under the Restatement (Second) of Torts, the essential elements of a cause of action for assistance and participation in the tort of the primary actor requires:

(1) the primary actor's activity to constitute a tort;
(2) the defendant to provide substantial assistance to the primary actor in accomplishing the tort; and
(3) the defendant's own conduct, separate from the primary actor's, to be a breach of duty to the plaintiff.

Restatement (Second) of Torts § 876(c), § 876(c) cmt. e.

(a) Primary Actor's Tort

As with a claim for assistance or encouragement, a claim for assistance and participation requires the primary actor to have committed a tort in the first place. *Id.* In order to prove that the defendant has assisted and participated in the primary actor's tort, the plaintiff first must show: (1) that the primary actor owed a duty to the plaintiff; and (2) that the primary actor breached this duty. *Kline*, 874 S.W.2d 786.

(b) Substantial Assistance

A claim for assistance and participation requires that the defendant provide the primary actor with substantial assistance in accomplishing the tort. Restatement (Second) of Torts § 876(c). Unlike liability for assistance or encouragement, encouragement is not enough to attach liability here. The finder of fact must find that the defendant assisted in the primary actor's tort. See *id.*

As with a claim for assistance or encouragement, a claim for assisting and participating requires the assistance given to the primary actor to be a substantial factor in causing the tort. Restatement (Second) of Torts § 876(c) cmt. e; compare § 876(b) cmt. d. It is possible that while a party's assistance and participation may be so slight as to not result in liability. *Id.* In determining whether the assistance and participation is a *substantial* factor in causing the tort, the court looks at five factors: (1) the nature of the act encouraged; (2) the amount of assistance given by the defendant; (3) the defendant's presence or absence at the time of the tort; (4) the defendant's relation to the primary actor; and (5) the defendant's state of mind. *Id*; *Juhl*, 936 S.W.2d at 644.

(c) Defendant's Participation in the Tort

A claim for assistance and participation requires that the defendant's own conduct, separate from the primary actor's, be a breach of duty to the plaintiff. *Id.* at § 876(c); see also, *City of Fort Worth*, 439 S.W.2d at 665. The plaintiff must therefore prove that a relationship exists between the plaintiff and the defendant that gives rise to a duty. In a case involving breach of a fiduciary duty, the defendant cannot be held liable unless a fiduciary relationship is present between the plaintiff and the defendant as well as between the plaintiff and the primary actor.

(2) Examples

(1) In *City of Fort Worth*, 439 S.W.2d at 665, defendant company, who owed plaintiff a fiduciary duty, was responsible for the acts of its employee, who participated in the primary actor's defrauding of plaintiff.

(2) In *Clayton v. Richards*, 47 S.W.3d 149, 154 (Tex. App.—Texarkana 2001, pet. denied), where the defendant, a private detective, assisted his client, the primary actor, in the installation of a video camera in the plaintiff's bedroom, defendant was jointly liable for the tort of invasion of privacy.

D. Concert of Action

Under the umbrella of aiding and abetting, Texas courts may also recognize an action for "concert of action." See *Gaulding v. Celotex Corp.*, 772 S.W.2d 66,

69 (Tex. 1989). Under concert of action, those who are in pursuit of a common plan or design to commit a tortious act and actively participate in it or lend aid, cooperation, or encouragement to the wrongdoer are equally liable. *Id.* (citing Prosser and Keeton on the Law of Torts § 46 (W. Keeton 5th ed. 1984 & Supp.1988)); Restatement (Second) of Torts § 876(a).

Whether Texas courts will recognize the concert of action theory of liability is "an open question." *Juhl*, 936 S.W.2d at 643. The *Gaulding* court expressly stated that their opinion was "not to be construed as approving or disapproving . . . concert of action . . . in an appropriate case," 772 S.W.2d at 71. Likewise, the *Juhl* court did not have the question of whether the cause of action was viable in front of it when the court discussed the theory. 936 S.W.2d at 644. Concert of action as it is defined in the Restatment (Second) of Torts as the codification of the common-law tort of mutual agency, § 876(a) cmt. a, which is a part of Texas common law. It therefore is a distinct possibility that the Texas Supreme Court will adopt a test similar to that found in the Restatement.

Concert of action is closely related to the civil conspiracy theory of liability, and in some cases the two terms are incorrectly used interchangeably. See *Pharo v. Smith*, 621 F.2d 656, 669 (5th Cir. 1980).

(1) Elements

In the *Juhl* opinion, the Texas Supreme Court recognizes the theory as defined in the Restatement, but notes that if the theory were adopted, Texas law would require the additional elements of specific intent and the presence of a highly dangerous activity. 936 S.W.2d at 645. As the theory would exist based on the *Juhl* opinion, the essential elements of a cause of action for concert of action would require:

(1) the defendant and another actor to commit an intentional tort;

(2) the tort to be a highly dangerous, deviant, or anti-social group activity likely to cause serious harm;

(3) the defendant to agree, explicitly or tacitly, to participate in the tort; and

(4) the defendant's own tortious conduct to cause the plaintiff's injury.

Juhl, 936 S.W.2d at 643-44; Restatement (Second) of Torts § 876(a).

(a) The Commission of an Intentional Tort

A claim for concert of action would require the defendant's, as well as the other actor's, commission of an intentional tort. *Juhl*, 936 S.W.2d at 645. A mere joint intent to engage in the conduct that resulted in the injury would not be sufficient. *Id.*; *Triplex Communications, Inc. v. Riley*, 900 S.W.2d 716, 719 (Tex. 1995). Like civil conspiracy, concert of action would require specific intent to agree "to accomplish an unlawful purpose or to accomplish a lawful purpose by unlawful means." *Juhl*, 936 S.W.2d at 644 (quoting *Triplex*, 900 S.W.2d at 719).

(b) A Highly Dangerous Tort

A claim for concert of action would require the tortious activity to be a highly dangerous, deviant, or anti-social group activity. *Juhl*, 936 S.W.2d at 645. Furthermore, this activity would have to be likely to cause either: (1) serious injury or death to a person; or (2) certain harm to a large number of people. *Id.*

This particular element is an outgrowth of the theory's history. The theory developed in cases in which innocent bystanders were injured during illegal drag races. It was developed as a means to hold the participants who were not in the cars that crashed liable. *Gaulding*, 772 S.W.2d at 69; see, e.g., *Bierczynski v. Rogers*, 239 A.2d 218 (Del. 1968); *Hood v. Evans*, 126 S.E.2d 898 (Ga. 1962).

(c) The Defendant's Agreement

A claim for concert of action would require the defendant to agree, either tacitly or explicitly, to the commission of the tort. *Juhl*, 936 S.W.2d at 643. It is not necessary for the plaintiff to directly prove agreement, or to prove existence of a physical agreement. Restatement (Second) of Torts § 876(a) cmt. a. The agreement can be inferred by the conduct of the parties, suggesting that the defendant either tacitly or explicitly agreed to the tortious conduct. *Id*; see, e.g., *Nelson v. Nason*, 177 N.E.2d 887, 888 (Mass. 1961).

(d) The Defendant's Tortious Conduct as Cause of the Injury

A claim for concert of action would require the defendant's own action to be tortious, and for this conduct to be a cause of the plaintiff's injury. Restatement (Second) of Torts § 876(a) cmt. c. One who innocently, rightfully, and carefully does an act that has the effect of furthering the tortious conduct or cooperating in the tortious design of another is not for that reason subject to liability. *Id.* A common plan, design, or express agreement alone will not result in concert of action liability; the defendants must participate in acts of a tortious character in carrying out the plan or agreement. *Gaulding*, 772 S.W.2d at 69. Furthermore, these tortious actions must be a cause of the plaintiff's injuries. Restatement (Second) of Torts § 876(a). However, unlike the theories of "assistance or encouragement" and "assistance and participation," the defendant's actions need not be a substantial factor in the commission of the tort in order for the defendant to be liable.

(2) Examples

(1) In *Payton v. Abbott Labs*, 512 F.Supp 1031, 1037-38 (D. Mass. 1981), the court acknowledged that if there was evidence the defendant and other pharmaceutical companies agreed not to test a drug used to prevent miscarriages in women to determine its safety, the defendant could be found liable under the concert of action theory.

(2) In *Nicolet, Inc. v. Nutt*, 525 A.2d 146 (Del. 1987), it was held that a cause of action exists against a party whose asbestos products did not cause the purported injury, but who allegedly conspired with other asbestos manufacturers to intentionally misrepresent and suppress relevant information regarding the health hazards of asbestos.

E. Texas Securities Act

The Texas Securities Act provides for a statutory aiding and abetting cause of action. The act states that a "person who directly or indirectly with intent to deceive or defraud or with reckless disregard for the truth or the law materially aids a seller, buyer, or issuer of a security is liable...jointly and severally with the seller, buyer, or issuer, and to the same extent as if he were the seller, buyer, or issuer. Tex. Rev. Civ. Stat. art. 581-33F(2)(Vernon Supp. 2005).

Under the federal Securities Exchange Act, no such aiding and abetting cause of action exists. See *Central Bank v. First Interstate Bank*, 511 U.S. 164, 176-77 (1994).

(1) Elements

The essential elements of a cause of action for aiding and abetting under the Texas Securities Act are:

(1) a primary actor's violation of the securities laws;

(2) the aider had general awareness of its role in this violation;

(3) the aider rendered substantial assistance in this violation; and

(4) the aider either intended to deceive plaintiff or acted with reckless disregard for the truth of the representations made by the primary violator.

Crescendo Invs. v. Brice, 61 S.W.3d 465, 472 (Tex. App.—San Antonio 2001, pet. denied).

(a) Violation of Securities Law

A claim for aiding and abetting under the Texas Securities Act requires a primary actor's violation of the securities laws. *Id.* According to the statute, as a threshold matter the primary actor must have violated either Section 33A, 33B, or 33C of the act. Tex. Rev. Civ. Stat. art. 581-33F(2). Section 33A deals with the liability of sellers, and states that a person who offers or sells a security in violation of the act is liable to the person buying the security from him. *Id.* at 581-33A. Section 33B deals with the liability of securities buyers, and states that a person who offers to buy or buys a security by means of an untrue statement of a material fact or an omission to state a material fact necessary in order to make the statements made not misleading, is liable to the person selling the security to him. *Id.* at 33B. Section 33C assigns liability to nonselling issuers who have registered if the prospectus that is filed along with the securities registration contains a falsehood or misleading statement. *Id.* at 33C.

(b) General Awareness

A claim for aiding and abetting under the Texas Securities Act requires the aider to have a general awareness of his role in the violation. *Crescendo Invs.*, 61 S.W.3d at 472. This element is not explicitly required by the statute, but has been required in many Texas courts. See *id.*; *Goldstein v. Mortenson*, 113 S.W.3d 769 (Tex. App.—Austin 2003, no pet.); *Frank v. Bear, Stearns & Co.*, 11 S.W.3d 380, 384 (Tex. App.—Houston [14th Dist.] 2000, pet. denied).

(c) Substantial Assistance

A claim for aiding and abetting under the Texas Securities Act requires the aider to render substantial assistance in the violation of the act. *Crescendo Invs.*, 61 S.W.3d at 472. What amounts to *substantial* assistance is highly fact-specific, and dependent on the nature of the primary violation as well as on the nature of the assistance. Cf. Lewis D. Lowenfels & Alan R. Bromberg, *A New Standard for Aiders and Abettors Under the Private Securities Litigation Reform Act of 1995*, 52 Bus. Law. 1, 1 (1996). Many courts will treat substantial assistance as a "causation concept" similar to the causation requirement for a primary violation. *Id.* The complaining party therefore may be required to prove that the actions and/or inactions of the alleged aider and abettor were a substantial, proximate causal factor of the primary violation and loss. *Id.*; See, e.g., *Metge v. Baehler*, 762 F.2d 621, 624 (8th Cir. 1985). Proof of a but-for causal relationship between the aider and abettor's actions and the primary actor's violation is not sufficient. *Id.*; *Bloor v. Carro, Spanbock, Londin, Rodman & Fass*, 754 F.2d 57, 63 (2d Cir. 1985).

(d) Intent or Reckless Disregard

A claim for aiding and abetting under the Texas Securities Act requires that the aider either intend to deceive the plaintiff or act with reckless disregard for the truth of the representations made by the primary actor. *Crescendo Invs.*, 61 S.W.3d at 472. This differs from the requirements for a claim against a party that has direct control over the primary actor, which do not require the plaintiff to prove intent or recklessness. Tex. Rev. Civ. Stat. Ann. art. 581-33F(1); *Busse v. Pac. Cattle Feeding Fund No. 1, Ltd.*, 896 S.W.2d 807, 815 (Tex. App.—Texarkana 1995, writ denied). If the plaintiff can prove that the controlled person violated one of the identified sections of the Texas Securities Act and that the defendant was a "control person" under the statute, then judgment against the defendant will be proper. *Id.* When the defendant is not in control of the primary actor, but is merely aiding or abetting the primary actor, intent or recklessness is required. Tex. Rev. Civ. Stat. Ann. art. 581-33F(2).

(2) Example

(1) In, *Goldstein*, 113 S.W.3d 769, where defendant helped the primary actor secure a loan in order to mask a deficit and mislead the plaintiffs, defendant was liable for materially aiding a seller of illegal securities under the Texas Securities Act.

F. Defenses

In a claim brought under any of the aiding and abetting theories, the defendant may use any defense that would apply to the underlying cause of action against the primary actor. Cf. *Cox v. Galena Park ISD*, 895 S.W.2d 745, 748-49 (Tex. App.—Corpus Christi 1994, no writ) (holding that the defendant's immunity defense barred the plaintiff's conspiracy claim).

G. Damages

As with civil conspiracy causes of action, the plaintiff in any aiding and abetting case is able to recover whatever damages are normally available for the underlying tort. *Tilton v. Marshall*, 925 S.W.2d 672, 681 (Tex. 1996). The plaintiff is required to establish that the damages suffered were proximately caused by the primary actor's underlying tort. *Insurance Co. of N. Am. v. Morris*, 981 S.W.2d 667, 675 (Tex. 1998).

Liability for aiding and abetting causes of action is joint and several. If damages are assessed jointly against the multiple aider-and-abettors, or against the aider-and-abettors and the primary actor, the parties will each be liable for payment of the entire amount of the damages. See *Carroll v. Timmers Chevrolet, Inc.*, 592 S.W.2d 922, 925-26 (Tex. 1979) (dealing with civil conspiracy). Once damages are assessed, the burden shifts to the defendants to apportion damages if the plaintiff can prove that: (1) all possible defendants are before the court, see *Gaulding*, 772 S.W.2d at 69, and; (2) the tortious conduct of multiple defendants combined to injure the plaintiff, *Celotex Corp v. Tate.*, 797 S.W.2d 197, 204 (Tex. App.—Corpus Christi 1990, writ dismissed by agreement).

II. BREACH OF FIDUCIARY DUTY

A. Introduction

B. Elements

    1) Existence of a Fiduciary Relationship

        (a) Relationships Where a Fiduciary Duty Is Recognized as a Matter of Law

            (i) Partners

            (ii) Joint Venturers

            (iii) Directors and Officers

            (iv) Brokers

            (v) Trustees and Executors

            (vi) Attorneys

        (b) Relationships Not Giving Rise to Fiduciary Duties

    (2) Breach of the Fiduciary Relationship
Damages

        (a) Restitution Types of Recovery

        (b) Constructive Trust

        (c) Mental Anguish Damages

        (d) Exemplary Damages

A. Introduction

The fiduciary duty, which is the highest duty recognized by law, contemplates good faith and fair dealing. *Wil-Roye Inv. Co. II v. Washington Mut. Bank, FA*, 142 S.W.3d 393, 409 (Tex. App.—El Paso 2004, no pet. h.). Moreover, a fiduciary must place the interests of the person to whom the duty is owed ahead of his own. *Id*. Once a fiduciary duty is established, there is a presumption that any transaction in favor of the fiduciary breaches that duty. See *National Plan Adm'rs, Inc. v. National Health Ins. Co.*, 150 S.W.3d 718, 733 (Tex.App.—Austin 2004, pet. granted). To overcome this presumption, the fiduciary must show that the transaction was fair. *Id*. This is traditionally a very fact-intensive question that is seldom resolved prior to trial. See *Chapman Children's Trust v. Porter & Hedges, LLP*, 32 S.W.3d 429, 439 (Tex. App.—Houston [14th Dist.] 2000, pet. denied).

B. Elements

1) Existence of a Fiduciary Relationship

Many formal fiduciary relationships are recognized as a matter of law, such as attorney/client, principal/agent, partners, joint venturers, and directors/shareholders. *Bohatch v. Butler & Binion,* 977 S.W.2d 543, 545 (Tex. 1998) (partners); *Kinzbach Tool Co. v. Corbett-Wallace Corp.,* 160 S.W.2d 509, 513 (Tex. 1942) (principal/agent); *Gibson v. Ellis,* 126 S.W.3d 324, 330 (Tex. App.—Dallas

2004, no pet. h.) (attorney/client); *Landon v. S&H Mktg. Group Inc.*, 82 S.W.3d 666, 672 (Tex. App.—Eastland 2002, no pet. h.) (directors/shareholders); *Fuqua v. Taylor*, 683 S.W.2d 735, 738 (Tex. App.—Dallas 1984, writ ref'd n.r.e.) (joint venturers). However, a fiduciary relationship is not limited to these legally recognized relationships. A "fiduciary" is "any person who occupies a position of peculiar confidence toward another, integrity and fidelity being implicit therein, with fair dealing and good faith rather than legal obligation as the basis of the transaction, and it includes those informal relations that exist whenever one party trusts and relies on another as well as technical fiduciary relations." 64 Tex. Jur. 3d *Restitution and Constructive Trusts* § 72 (2003).

Confidential relationships may also be recognized where "influence has been acquired and abused, [or] in which confidence has been reposed and betrayed." *Tex. Bank & Trust Co. v. Moore*, 595 S.W.2d 502, 507 (Tex. 1980). The origin of the confidence may be moral, social, domestic, or merely personal. *Id.*; see *also Associated Indem. Corp. v. CAT Contracting, Inc.*, 964 S.W.2d 276, 287 (Tex. 1998). "A confidential relationship exists where one person has a special confidence in another to the extent that the parties do not deal with each other equally, either because of dominance on one side or weakness, dependence, or justifiable trust on the other." *Pope v. Darcey*, 667 S.W.2d 270, 275 (Tex. App.—Houston [14th Dist.] 1984, writ ref'd n.r.e.) (citation omitted).

Not every relationship involving a high degree of trust and confidence, however, will give rise to a fiduciary relationship. *Schlumberger Tech. Corp. v. Swanson*, 959 S.W.2d 171, 176-77 (Tex. 1997). In *Schlumberger*, the

Texas Supreme Court held that mere subjective trust did not, as a matter of law, transform arms-length dealings into a fiduciary relationship. *Id.* Rather, the relationship must exist prior to, and apart from, the agreement made the basis of the suit. *Id.;* see also *Associated Indem. Corp.,* 964 S.W.2d at 288. Absent evidence of a preexisting confidential relationship between parties, the court will not impose a fiduciary duty in a business transaction. *Schlumberger,* 959 S.W.2d at 176-77.

(a) Relationships Where a Fiduciary Duty Is Recognized as a Matter of Law

(i) Partners

The "relationship between . . . partners . . . is fiduciary in character, and imposes upon all the participants the obligation of loyalty to the joint concern and of the utmost good faith, fairness, and honesty in their dealings with each other with respect to the matters pertaining to the enterprise." *Bohatch,* 977 S.W.2d at 545. One source of these obligations is the Texas Revised Partnership Act ("TRPA"), which provides that a partner owes to the partnership and the other partners a duty of loyalty, care and good faith. Tex. Rev. Civ. Stat. Ann. art. 6132b-4.04 (Vernon 2004).

The partnership agreement may establish standards controlling the extent of these duties among partners, but the partnership agreement may not eliminate the statutory duties all together. Tex. Rev. Civ. Stat. 6132b-1.03(a) & (b) (Vernon 2004). At the heart of the partnership concept is the principle that partners may choose with whom they wish to be associated. *Bohatch,* 977 S.W.2d at 545. The fiduciary duties that partners owe one another do not encompass a duty to remain partners. *Id.*

Further, although the Texas Revised Partnership Act was intended to bring partnership law in line with modern business practices, including a rejection of the standard "fiduciary" label, cases still carry over the strict fiduciary language. See, e.g., *Brosseau v. Ranzau,* 81 S.W.3d 381, 394-95 (Tex. App.—Beaumont 2002, pet. denied) (partners owe one another a fiduciary duty, included in which is a strict duty of good faith, while a managing partner owes his partners the highest duty recognized in law).

(ii) Joint Venturers

Like partners, joint venturers owe a fiduciary duty toward one another. *Fuqua,* 683 S.W.2d at 738 (citing *Rankin v. Naftalis,* 557 S.W.2d 940 (Tex. 1979)). The terms of a contract between joint venturers control the extent of the "fiduciary" duties between the parties. *Id.*

To have a joint venture, there must be: (1) a community of interest in the venture/partnership; (2) an agreement to share profits; (3) an agreement to share losses; and (4) a mutual right to control or manage the enterprise. *Baskin v. Mortgage & Trust Inc.,* 837 S.W.2d 743, 747 (Tex. App.—Houston [14th Dist.] 1992, writ denied) (citation omitted). Absent a contract reflecting each of these elements, no fiduciary duty arises.

For instance, in *Stephanz v. Laird,* the trial court awarded the plaintiff tort damages based, in part, on breach of fiduciary duty. 846 S.W.2d 895, 897 (Tex. App.—Houston [1st Dist.] 1993, writ denied). However, the appellate court held the contract did not create a partnership agreement, but a contract for employment from which tort damages based on a breach of fiduciary duty could not flow. *Id.* at 900.

(iii) Directors and Officers

Corporate fiduciaries include key corporate employees, directors and officers, as well as shareholders under certain circumstances. The Texas Supreme Court has defined the duties of an officer or director as corporate fiduciaries:

> A corporate fiduciary is under obligation not to usurp corporate opportunities for personal gain, and equity will hold him accountable to the corporation for his profits if he does so. Transactions, in which a corporate fiduciary derives personal profit, either in dealing with the corporation or its property, or in matters of corporate interest, are subject to the closest examination and the form of the transaction will give way to the substance of what actually has been brought about.

International Bankers Life Ins. Co. v. Holloway, 368 S.W.2d 567, 577 (Tex. 1963); *Landon,* 82 S.W.3d at 672. However, the right to recover for a corporate breach of fiduciary duty belongs to the corporation, not the corporate shareholders, regardless of whether the shareholders have been directly or indirectly harmed by that action. *Wingate v. Hajdik*, 795 S.W.2d 717, 719 (Tex. 1990).

The Texas Legislature has enacted legislation with respect to interested director transactions. Tex. Bus.

Corp. Act Ann. art. 2.35-1 (Vernon Supp. 2004). The statute provides that an interested director's contract or transaction can be validated if: (1) the material facts as to the interested director's relationship or interest and as to the contract or transaction are disclosed and the board or committee authorizes the contract or transaction by the affirmative vote of a majority of the disinterested directors; (2) the material facts as to the relationship or interest and as to the contract or transaction are disclosed and the contract or transaction is specifically approved in good faith by vote of the shareholders; or (3) the contract or transaction is fair as to the corporation at the time it is authorized, approved, or ratified by the board of directors, a committee thereof, or the shareholders. Tex. Bus. Corp. Act Ann. art. 2.35-1 (Vernon Supp. 2004). "It appears that this statute alters common law with respect to the requirement that the director prove that the contract or transaction is fair to the corporation for every challenged transaction." *Landon,* 82 S.W.3d at 673.

Examples of Texas cases alleging breach of fiduciary duty by an officer, director, or controlling owner of a corporate entity are as follows:

> (1)   Corporation recovered against officers for usurping corporate opportunity by purchasing property that was useful to the corporation's operations and then leasing the property to the corporation in order to finance a $100,000 profit. *General Dynamics v. Torres*, 915 S.W.2d 45 (Tex. App.—El Paso 1995, writ denied);
>
> (2)   Minority shareholder recovers against the majority shareholder for usurping corporate

opportunity by taking a right of first refusal on a purchase in his own name and for an inaccurate division of the return of capital distributions at the close of business. *Thywissen v. Cron*, 781 S.W.2d 682 (Tex. App.—Houston [1st Dist.] 1989, writ denied);

(3) Creditor held to have a cause of action for breach of fiduciary duty if corporate transfers made to defraud creditors or to allow corporation to become insolvent. *Dyer v. Shafer, Gilliland, Davis, McCollum & Ashley, Inc.*, 779 S.W.2d 474, 477 (Tex. App.—El Paso 1989, writ denied) (citing *In re Safety Int'l, Inc.*, 775 F.2d 660 (5th Cir. 1985));

(4) Minority shareholder of closely held corporation could bring derivative suit against remaining shareholders for their failure to include him in a subsequently formed corporation performing substantially the same business activities as the prior corporation. *Eye Site, Inc. v. Blackburn*, 796 S.W.2d 160 (Tex. 1990);

(5) Court denied claim by a salaried corporate officer for compensation from another corporation, where the officer was expected to devote his full energies for the sole benefit of his employer corporation. *In re Westec Corp.*, 434 F.2d 195 (5th Cir. 1970).

(iv) Brokers

Real estate brokers, as agents, are fiduciaries to their principals. *Southern Cross Indus., Inc. v. Martin*, 604

S.W.2d 290, 292 (Tex. Civ. App.—San Antonio 1980, writ ref'd n.r.e.). In *Southern Cross Industries*, the appellate court upheld a principal's defense against a real estate broker's claim for a fee because the broker, acting as a potential buyer, did not disclose all the pertinent facts regarding other buyers for the property to the principal. *Id.* at 293. Thus, when the principal sold to another buyer, the broker could not recover a fee. *Id.*

Similarly, securities brokers owe a fiduciary duty to their customers in matters within the scope of their agency. *Hand v. Dean Witter Reynolds Inc.,* 889 S.W.2d 483, 493 n.5 (Tex. App.—Houston [14th Dist.] 1994, writ denied). To determine what fiduciary duty a broker owes to its customer, the court will examine the relationship between the broker and the customer. *Martinez Tapia v. Chase Manhattan Bank, N.A.,* 149 F.3d 404, 412 (5th Cir. 1998). For example, if the customer controls a nondiscretionary account and retains the ability to make investment decisions, the broker's fiduciary duty is limited to executing the customer's order. *Romano v. Merill Lynch, Pierce, Fenner & Smith,* 834 F.2d 523, 530 (5th Cir. 1987); see also *Edward D. Jones & Co. v. Fletcher*, 975 S.W.2d 539, 544 (Tex. 1998) (broker had no fiduciary duty to ascertain elderly customer's mental capacity before assisting customer in transferring securities); *Anton v. Merill Lynch*, 36 S.W.3d 251, 256-58 (Tex. App.—Austin 2001, pet. denied) (investment firm had no fiduciary duty to inform a spouse of a change in beneficiary, even though she was also their client). With a discretionary account, the broker is responsible for making investment decisions as well as managing the account. *Hand,* 889 S.W.2d at 493 n.5. Thus, the broker's fiduciary duty would not be confined to executing the orders he has accepted from the customer; the duty would be broader. See *id.*

(v) Trustees and Executors

Trustees and executors have general and specific fiduciary duties, imposed both by common law and the Texas Trust Code, regarding the management and investment of trust assets. Tex. Prop. Code Ann. § 113.051 et. seq (Vernon 2004); see also *Huie v. DeShazo*, 922 S.W.2d 920, 923 (Tex. 1996) (quoting *Montgomery v. Kennedy*, 669 S.W.2d 309, 313 (Tex. 1984)) (trustees and executors owe beneficiaries a fiduciary duty of full disclosure of all material facts known to them that might affect the beneficiaries' rights).

(vi) Attorneys

An attorney's fiduciary duty to his client involves the "integrity and fidelity" of an attorney and focuses on whether the attorney obtained an improper benefit from representing his client. *Gibson,* 126 S.W.3d at 330. "An attorney breaches his fiduciary duty when he benefits improperly from the attorney-client relationship by, among other things, subordinating his client's interest to his own, retaining the client's funds, engaging in self-dealing, improperly using client confidences, failing to disclose conflicts of interest, or making misrepresentations to achieve these ends." *Id.* (citing *Goffney v. Rabson,* 56 S.W.3d 186, 193 (Tex.App.—Houston [14th Dist.] 2001, pet. denied)).

(b) Relationships Not Giving Rise to Fiduciary Duties

Certain relationships do not give rise to a fiduciary duty as a matter of law. For instance, businessmen do not owe fiduciary duties to each other in a general arms-length transaction. In *Kline v. O'Quinn*, the appellate court held that an attorney who had a written agreement with another attorney for the division of settlement proceeds did not have a fiduciary relationship. 874 S.W.2d 776, 785-86 (Tex. App.—Houston [14th Dist.] 1994, writ denied). The court reasoned:

> The fact that one businessman trusts another, and relies upon his promise to perform a contract does not rise to a confidential relationship. Every contract includes an element of confidence and trust that each party will faithfully perform his obligation under the contract. Neither is the fact that the relationship has been a cordial one, of long duration, evidence of a confidential relationship.

Id. (citing *Crim*, 823 S.W.2d at 594-95). "A fiduciary relationship is [an] [sic] extraordinary one and will not be lightly created...." *Kline*, 874 S.W.2d at 786. Simply because one party trusts another does not alone create a fiduciary relationship. *Id.* Rather, as discussed above, the relationship must exist prior to, and apart from, the transaction between the parties. *Id.;* see *Associated Indem. Corp.*, 964 S.W.2d at 288.

Similarly, the relationship between a borrower and its lender generally does not create a fiduciary duty. *Federal Deposit Ins. Corp. v. Coleman*, 795 S.W.2d 706, 708-09 (Tex. 1990); *Berry v. First Nat'l Bank of Olney*, 894 S.W.2d 558, 560 (Tex. App.—Fort Worth 1995, no writ). Instead, to impose a fiduciary duty on a lender, a borrower must demonstrate a "special and confidential relationship" between the borrower and lender. For example, the appellate court in *Farah v. Mafrige & Kormanik, P.C.* stated that "when a special relationship between a borrow and lender has been found, it has rested on extraneous facts and conduct, such as excessive lender control over, or influence in, the borrower's business activities." 927 S.W.2d 663, 675 (Tex. App.—Houston [1st Dist.] 1996, no writ) (citation omitted).

(2) Breach of the Fiduciary Relationship

A fiduciary breaches the relationship by committing acts that benefit him or her rather than the party to whom the fiduciary duty is owed. *Collins v. Smith*, 53 S.W.3d 832, 840 (Tex. App.—Houston [1st Dist.] 2001, no pet.); see also *Southwest Livestock & Trucking Co. v. Dooley*, 884 S.W.2d 805, 809 (Tex. App.—San Antonio 1994, writ denied). In certain cases, a fiduciary breaches his duty even if the party to whom the fiduciary duty is owed is not damaged. *Burrow v. Arce,* 997 S.W.2d 229, 238 (Tex. 1999) (client does not have to prove actual damages to obtain forfeiture of attorney's fees due to attorney's breach of fiduciary duties).

Further, the existence of the fiduciary relationship may make non-disclosure of material facts a breach. The fiduciary must "deal openly" and "make full disclosure to the party with whom he stands in such relationship." *Kinzbach Tool Co., Inc. v. Corbett-Wallace Corp.*, 160 S.W.2d 509, 513 (Tex. 1942). "It is the law in such instances if the fiduciary takes any gift, gratuity, or benefit in violation of his duty, or acquires an interest adverse to his principal, without full disclosure, it is a betrayal of his trust and a breach of confidence . . . " *Johnson v. Brewer & Prichard, P.C.,* 73 S.W.3d 193, 200-201 (Tex. 2002) (citations omitted).

Finally, Texas courts have applied a presumption of unfairness to transactions between a fiduciary and a party to whom he owes a fiduciary duty, thereby, shifting the burden of proof upon the fiduciary defendant to prove that the transaction in question is fair. *Texas Bank & Trust Co. v. Moore*, 595 S.W.2d 502, 508-09 (Tex. 1980); *Collins,* 53 S.W.3d at 840. Specifically, the "fiduciary must show proof of good faith and that the transaction was fair, honest, and equitable." *Collins*, 53 S.W.3d at 840 (citation omitted).

(3) Damages

(a) *Restitution Types of Recovery*

A fiduciary who breaches a fiduciary duty may be ordered to pay restitution damages, which may include a reduced fee or forfeiture of a fee already paid or profits earned. An attorney who commits a clear and serious breach of his fiduciary duty to his client may be required to forfeit some or all of his fees as long as the client has pled the equitable remedy of fee forfeiture. *Burrow,* 997 S.W.2d at 241; *Lee v. Lee,* 47 S.W.3d 767, 780-81 (Tex. App.—Houston [14th Dist.] 2001, pet. denied). Profits are recoverable when they were realized by the fiduciary at the expense of the beneficiary. *Int'l Bankers Life Ins. Co.,* 368 S.W.2d at 577-78; *Carr v. Weiss*, 984 S.W.2d 753, 769-70 (Tex. App.—Amarillo 1999, pet. denied); *Russell v. Truitt,* 554 S.W.2d 948, 955 (Tex. Civ. App.—Fort Worth 1977, writ ref'd n.r.e.). Plaintiffs may also recover accompanying carrying costs such as tax, interest, maintenance, and insurance. *NRC, Inc. v. Huddleston,* 886 S.W.2d 526, 531 (Tex. App.—Austin 1994, no writ).

(b) Constructive Trust

A plaintiff in a breach of fiduciary duty case may be entitled to an equitable remedy, such as the creation of a constructive trust. A constructive trust arises when the legal title to property is obtained by a person in violation of an express or implied duty owed to one who has an equitable interest in the property. *Fitz-Gerald v. Hull,* 237 S.W.2d 256, 262 (Tex. 1951). Thus, in order to prevent unjust enrichment of the legal holder, such person is deemed to hold the property as a trustee for the beneficial use of that party which has been wrongfully deprived of its rights. *Id.*; see also *Mims v. Beall,* 810 S.W.2d 876, 881-82 (Tex. App.—Texarkana 1991, no writ) (constructive trust placed on proceeds of oil and gas production to protect royalty rights of nonparticipating interest owner).

(c) Mental Anguish Damages

Mental damages can be awarded for breach of fiduciary duty if the damages are a foreseeable result of the breach. *Douglas v. Delp,* 987 S.W.2d 879, 885 (Tex. 1999); see, e.g., *Perez v. Kirk & Carrigan,* 822 S.W.2d 261, 266-67 (Tex. App.—Corpus Christi 1991, writ denied) (mental anguish damages were appropriate for lawyer's breach of confidentiality which resulted in public embarrassment of former client).

(d) Exemplary Damages

Exemplary damages for breach of fiduciary duty are proper when the breach is intentional or the fiduciary has engaged in self-dealing. *Hawthorne v. Guenther*, 917 S.W.2d 924, 936 (Tex. App.—Beaumont 1996, writ denied). Exemplary damages may also be available for a breach of fiduciary duty committed through fraud or with malicious intent. Tex. Civ. Prac. & Rem. Code § 41.003 (Vernon 2004). For cases filed on or after September 1, 2003, the plaintiff may recover exemplary damages upon a showing of clear and convincing evidence that the harm on which the suit is based resulted from the fiduciary's fraud or malice. Tex. Civ. Prac. & Rem. Code § 41.003. Chapter 41 defines "fraud" as fraud other than constructive fraud and "malice" as a specific intent by the defendant to cause substantial injury or harm to the claimant. Tex. Civ. Prac. & Rem. Code §§ 41.001(6) & (7).

Furthermore, exemplary damages may only be awarded where there is unanimity in the jury findings. Both Civil Practice and Remedies Code § 41.003(d) and Texas Rule of Civil Procedure 292, which became effective on February 1, 2005, provide that exemplary damages may be awarded only if the jury was unanimous in finding liability and the amount of exemplary damages. Therefore, a plaintiff must obtain a unanimous finding by all twelve jurors for both liability and the amount of exemplary damages.

III. CIVIL CONSPIRACY

A. Introduction

The Texas Supreme Court has repeatedly defined civil conspiracy as a combination by two or more persons to accomplish an unlawful purpose or to accomplish a lawful purpose by unlawful means. See *J.T.T. v. Chon Tri,* 162 S.W.3d 552, 556 (Tex. 2005); see also *Triplex Comm., Inc. v. Riley,* 900 S.W.2d 716, 719-20 (Tex. 1995); see also *Massey v. Armco Steel Co.,* 652 S.W.2d 932, 934 (Tex. 1983); see also *Carroll v. Timmers Chevrolet, Inc.,* 592 S.W.2d 922, 925 (Tex. 1979); see also *Schlumberger Well Surveying Corp. v. Nortex Oil & Gas Corp.,* 435 S.W.2d 854, 856 (Tex. 1968); see also *Great Nat'l Life Ins. Co. v. Chapa,* 377 S.W.2d 632, 635 (Tex. 1964).

The essence of a cause of action for conspiracy is damage from the commission of a wrong which injured another, not the conspiracy itself. *Triplex,* 900 S.W.2d at 720; see also *Estate of Stonecipher v. Estate of Butts,* 591 S.W.2d 806, 808 (Tex. 1980); see also *Schlumberger,* 435 S.W.2d at 856. The significance of an action for civil conspiracy is that one individual defendant may be held liable for the actions of another defendant, if those actions constitute a tort or other legal wrong, solely as a result of the proof of a conspiracy.

B. Elements of Conspiracy

The essential elements of a cause of action for civil conspiracy are:

(1) two or more persons;
(2) an object to be accomplished;
(3) a meeting of the minds on the object or course of action;
(4) one or more unlawful, overt acts; and
(5) damages as the proximate result.

J.T.T., 162 W.W. 3d at 556; see also *Ins. Co. of N. Am. v. Morris,* 981 S.W.2d 667, 675 (Tex. 1998); *Massey,* 652 S.W.2d at 934; see also *San Antonio Credit Union v. O'Connor,* 115 S.W.3d 82, 90 (Tex. App.—San Antonio 2003, pet. denied); see also *Trostle v. Trostle,* 77 S.W.3d 908, 915 (Tex. App.—Amarillo 2002, no pet.); see also *Christensen v. Sherwood Ins. Servs.,* 758 S.W.2d 801, 804 (Tex. App.—Texarkana 1988, writ denied); see also *Garcia v. C.F. Jordan, Inc.,* 881 S.W.2d 155, 157 (Tex. App.—El Paso 1994, no writ).

(1) Two or More Persons

A claim for civil conspiracy requires a combination of two or more persons or entities. See *Firestone Steel Prods. Co. v. Barajas,* 927 S.W.2d 608, 614 (Tex. 1996); *Berry v. Golden Light Coffee Co.,* 327 S.W.2d 436, 440 (Tex. 1959). Accordingly, a single entity cannot conspire with itself. *Fisher v. Yates,* 953 S.W.2d 370, 382 (Tex. App.—Texarkana 1997, pet. denied, 988 S.W.2d 730 (Tex.1988)(*per curium*)). So while two or more businesses can conspire with each other, a corporation cannot conspire with itself, no matter how many of its agents participate in the act. *Berry,* 327 S.W.2d at 440; *Fojtik v. First Nat'l Bank of Beeville,* 752 S.W.2d 669, 673 (Tex. App.—Corpus Christi 1988), *writ denied,* 775 S.W.2d 632 (Tex. 1989) (*per curium*); *Bayou Terrace Inv. Corp.*

v. Lyles, 881 S.W.2d 810, 815 (Tex. App.—Houston [1st Dist.] 1994, no writ). There is a split between districts concerning whether a corporation can conspire with its wholly-owned subsidiary. Compare *Atlantic Richfield Co. v. Misty Prods., Inc.*, 820 S.W.2d 414, 420 (Tex. App.—Houston [14th Dist.] 1991, writ denied) (holding that a conspiracy cannot exist between a corportion and its wholly-owned subsidiary) with *Grizzle v. Texas Commerce Bank*, 38 S.W.3d 265 284 (Tex. App.—Dallas 2001), (rev'd on other grounds), 96 S.W.3d 246 (Tex 2002) (holding that a corporation and its wholly owned subsidiary, as separate entities can enter into a conspiracy).

(2) Object of Conspiracy

A claim for civil conspiracy requires that the object of the combination was to accomplish an unlawful purpose or a lawful purpose by unlawful means. *Ernst & Young, L.L.P. v. Pacific Mut. Life Ins. Co.*, 51 S.W.3d 573, 583 (Tex. 2001); see also *Morris*, 981 S.W.2d at 675; see also *Triplex*, 900 S.W.2d at 719. This is because a defendant's liability for conspiracy depends on participation in some underlying tort for which the plaintiff seeks to hold at least one of the named defendants liable. *Tilton v. Marshall*, 925 S.W.2d 672, 681 (Tex. 1996). No actionable conspiracy exists if the purpose or object of a conspiracy is lawful and the conspirators have a legitimate purpose to serve by their actions and conduct, even if the actions are motivated by malice. *First State Bank v. Keilman*, 851 S.W.2d 914, 925-26 (Tex. App.—Austin 1993, writ denied); see also *Bates v. Fuller*, 663 S.W.2d 512, 517-18 (Tex. App.—Tyler 1983, no writ). As a result, a plaintiff cannot prevail on a conspiracy claim if the defendants are not liable for some underlying tort. See *Tilton*, 925 S.W.2d at 681.

(3) Meeting of Minds

A claim for civil conspiracy requires the conspirators to have a meeting of the minds about the object of their conspiracy. *Massey*, 652 S.W.2d at 934. A meeting of the minds is an agreement or understanding between the conspirators to inflict a wrong on another. *O'Connor*, 115 S.W.3d at 90. Therefore, the participants must have specific intent or an awareness of the wrongful conduct that is the object of the conspiracy at the inception of the combination or agreement. *Triplex*, 900 S.W.2d at 719. One cannot agree, either expressly or tacitly, to the commission of a wrong of which he is not aware. See *Schlumberger*, 435 S.W.2d at 857. Accordingly, a person or entity cannot inadvertently become a member of a civil conspiracy. *Berstein v. Portland Sav. and Loan Ass'n.*, 850 S.W.2d 694, 705-06 (Tex. App.—Corpus Christi 1993, writ denied). As a result, parties cannot engage in a civil conspiracy to be negligent. *Reed Tool Co. v. Copelin*, 689 S.W.2d 404, 406 (Tex. 1985).

(4) Overt Acts

To have a successful claim for civil conspiracy, the plaintiff must establish that an unlawful overt act was committed in furtherance of the conspiracy. *Massey*, 652 S.W.2d at 934. A mere agreement to enter into some wrongful act does not amount to a tort or constitute civil conspiracy; there must be some act committed by one or more of the conspirators to advance, pursue or implement their agreement. See *Triplex*, 900 S.W.2d at 719.

(5) Damages

A civil conspiracy claim requires a plaintiff to establish that it suffered damages as a proximate result of the wrongful act involved in the conspiracy. *Ins. Co. of N. Am.* v. *Morris*, 981 S.W.2d 667, 675 (Tex. 1998); *Massey*, 652 S.W.2d at 934. It is the damages resulting from a wrongful act, not the agreement itself, which gives rise to a cause of action for civil conspiracy. *Coppock & Teltschik v. Mayor, Day & Caldwell*, 857 S.W.2d 631, 640 (Tex. App.—Houston [1st Dist.] 1993, writ denied). If no damage arises out of the agreement to commit a wrongful act, a cause of action for civil conspiracy will not lie. *Wavell v. Roberts*, 818 S.W.2d 462, 465 (Tex. App.—Corpus Christi 1991, writ denied). Accordingly, the mere fact of proving the conspiracy itself is not a recoverable harm. *Schlumberger*, 435 S.W.2d at 856.

(a) Actual Damages

Recovery for civil conspiracy is based upon the injury caused by the underlying tort. *Tilton*, 925 S.W.2d at 681. As a result, plaintiffs must look to the underlying tort to determine what damages are available. For recovery of actual damages, a plaintiff can recover whatever actual damages are available for the underlying tort. *Id.*

(b) Exemplary Damages

A plaintiff can recover exemplary damages if the underlying tort allows for exemplary damages. See, e.g., *Akin v. Dahl*, 661 S.W.2d 917, 921 (Tex. 1983); see also *Goldstein v. Mortenson*, 113 S.W.3d 769, 782 (Tex. App.—Austin 2003, no pet.); see also *Hart v. Moore,* 952 S.W.2d 90, 98 (Tex. App.—Amarillo 1997, pet. denied). However, recovery of exemplary damages requires a finding of an independent tort with accompanying actual damages. *Schlueter v. Schlueter*, 975 S.W.2d 584, 589 (Tex. 1998).

(c) Lost Profits

Texas courts have allowed recovery of lost profits in civil conspiracy cases. See *Commodity Credit Corp v. Transit Grain Co.,* 157 F. Supp. 527, 538 (S.D. Tex. 1957); *Nix v. Born,* 870 S.W.2d 635, 639 (Tex. App.—El Paso 1994, no writ); see also *Horton v. Robinson,* 776 S.W.2d 260, 263 (Tex. App.—El Paso 1989, no writ). These courts followed the guidelines for the recovery of lost profits set forth by the Texas Supreme Court in *Holt Atherton Indus., Inc. v. Heine,* 835 S.W.2d 80, 84 (Tex. 1992), namely: (1) recovery for lost profits does not require that the loss be susceptible of exact calculation, but the amount of the loss must be shown by competent evidence with reasonable certainty; (2) the opinions or estimates of lost profits must be based on objective data from which the amount of lost profits can be ascertained; and (3) it is not necessary to produce in court the documents supporting the opinions or estimates. *Id.*

(d) Out-of-Pocket and Consequential Damages

At least one Texas court has allowed a plaintiff to recover out-of-pocket expenses and consequential damages as "damages naturally flowing from a civil conspiracy." *Operation Rescue Nat'l v. Planned Parenthood,* 937 S.W.2d 60, 83 (Tex. App.—Houston [14th Dist.] 1996), *aff'd as modified,* 975 S.W.2d 546 (Tex. 1998) (affirming trial court's award for costs associated with increased security and safety measures in a case involving property damages in connection with protest activities).

(e) Mental Anguish Damages

Mental anguish damages are recoverable against civil conspirators under proper circumstances. See *St. Louis & S.W.R.Y. Co. of Texas v. Chapa,* 113 S.W. 144, 146 (Tex. 1908). In a case involving an award of mental anguish damages to a civil conspiracy plaintiff, the Fifth Circuit Court stated, "[t]he wrongs committed in the instant case fall within the Texas rule that damages are recoverable for mental suffering unaccompanied by physical suffering when the wrong complained of is a willful one intended by the wrongdoer to produce mental anguish or from which result could be reasonably anticipated as a natural consequence." *Fenslage v. Dawkins,* 629 F.2d 1107, 1110 (5th Cir. 1980) (citing *Stafford v. Steward,* 295 S.W.2d 665, 667 (Tex. Civ. App. 1956, writ dism'd by agr.); see also *Nix v. Born,* 870 S.W.2d 635, 642 (Tex. App.—El Paso 1994, no writ) (testimony that being emotionally "hurt" and having mental anguish did not rise to the level required for recovery).

(f) Disgorgement of Defendant's Profits

To prevent conspirators from being unjustly enriched, at least one court has awarded the defendants' profit to the plaintiff. See *Commodity Credit Corp.,* 157 F. Supp. at 538. The court entered judgment by disgorging profits from the defendants that they received by fraudulently conspiring to give one company preferential treatment at the expense of other companies. *Id.* at 540.

C. Proof of Conspiracy

Texas courts recognize that conspirators are unlikely to admit to the conspiracy; thus, proof of conspiracy will most often be made by circumstantial evidence. However, the vital facts may not be proven by unreasonable inferences from other facts and circumstances or by inferences piled on inferences. See *Schlumberger*, 435 S.W.2d at 856; see also *Kirby*, 688 S.W.2d at 164. The evidence must do more than raise a suspicion of a conspiracy. *Carr v. Hunt*, 651 S.W.2d 875, 882 (Tex. App.—Dallas 1983, writ ref'd n.r.e.). Furthermore, if any one or more of the circumstantial facts are as consistent with a lawful purpose as they are with an unlawful undertaking, those facts are insufficient to establish a conspiracy. See e.g., *Bohn v. Travelers Indem. Co.*, 604 S.W.2d 327, 330 (Tex. Civ. App.—Texarkana 1980, no writ).

D. Liable Parties

If a civil conspiracy is proven, each of the parties to the conspiracy is responsible for all acts done by any of the conspirators in furtherance of the conspiracy. See *Berry*, 327 S.W.2d at 438. Accordingly, conspirators are jointly and severally liable for all damages. See e.g., *Carroll*, 592 S.W.2d at 926; *Hart*, 952 S.W.2d at 98; *Kirby*, 688 S.W.2d at 164.

E. Examples

(1) In *Remenchik v. Whittington*, 757 S.W.2d 836 (Tex. App.—Houston [14th Dist.] 1988, no writ), the court found that a construction contractor was liable for civil

conspiracy when it conspired with a general partner to defraud limited partners from profits arising from a construction project.

(2) In *Horton v. Robinson*, 776 S.W.2d 260 (Tex. App.—El Paso 1989, no writ), the court found a promoter was liable for civil conspiracy when he conspired with second promoter to breach the second promoter's fiduciary duty to third promoter by not distributing to him his share of the corporation's profits.

IV. Defamation of a Business Entity and Business Disparagement

A. Introduction

B. Defamation of a Business Entity

   (1) Proper Plaintiffs

   (2) Proper Defendants

   (3) Definition and Elements

      (a) Statement Must be Defamatory

      (b) Publication to Third Parties

      (c) Intentional or Negligent Publication

      (d) Actual Damages or Per Se Defamatory

   (4) Privileges

      (a) Section 73.002 Privilege

      (b) Common-Law Absolute Privilege

      (c) Common-Law Qualified Privilege

   (5) Remedies

      (a) Actual/General Damages

      (b) Special Damages

      (c) Exemplary Damages

      (d) Special Mitigation of Damages Rules

A. Introduction

Defamation of a business entity and business disparagement are two separate torts. Each has separate consequences and considerations for the business owner. An action for defamation arises when reputation is the subject of the criticism; therefore, the action protects the reputation of the injured party. Restatement (Second) of Torts § 623A, cmt. g (1977). Whereas, an action for business disparagement arises when products or services of a business are the subject of criticism; therefore, the action protects against pecuniary loss. *Id.* More specifically, in an action for defamation of a business entity, the damages alleged in the case are primarily personal and general (for example, injury to the owner's personal reputation) even though incidental or consequential professional losses can also be pleaded and proved. See *Williamson v. New Times, Inc.*, 980 S.W.2d 706, 710-11 (Tex. App.—Fort Worth 1998, no pet.). However, in an action for business disparagement, the damages alleged are limited to business or property losses, even though aspects of injury to reputation may be incidentally involved. See *id.* The injured party may sue for both torts in the same suit as long as duplication of damages is avoided. *Id.*

B. Defamation of a Business Entity

(1) Proper Plaintiffs

In an action for defamation of a business entity, the plaintiff must establish standing on the type of entity involved. When the business is unincorporated, the owner is the proper plaintiff to bring claims for defamation to the business. See *Cranberg v. Consumers Union of U.S., Inc.*, 756 F.2d 382, 389 (5th Cir. 1985), *cert. denied,* 474 U.S. 850 (1985); *Miller v. Reinert,* 534 S.W.2d 161, 163 (Tex. Civ. App.—Waco 1976, writ dism'd w.o.j.). The owner may recover individually only if he or she is so closely associated with the business that an alleged defamation of the business name also refers by implication to the owner. *Id.* Identification of the independent owner with the business need not be in the mind of the general public, but the association is sufficient if those who know or are acquainted with the owner understand from reading the publication that it refers to him or her. *Outlet Co. v. Int'l Sec. Group, Inc.*, 693 S.W.2d 621, 625-26 (Tex. App.—San Antonio 1985, writ ref'd n.r.e.).

When the business is a corporation, the corporation is the proper plaintiff, provided that the corporation is identified sufficiently in the allegedly libelous statement. *Gen. Motors Acceptance Corp. v. Howard*, 487 S.W.2d 708, 712-13 (Tex. 1972). Similar to an unincorporated business, an individual, who is so closely identified with the corporation that she acts for the corporation, may also recover individually. *Id.* The libelous statement must refer, either directly or through an ownership association, to a particular individual, corporation or other entity, and reference to a group of persons or entities cannot be the basis for a libel action. *Webb v. Sessions*, 531 S.W.2d 211, 212-13 (Tex. Civ. App.—Eastland 1975, no writ). An exception is made in unusual situations, such as when a corporation's entire management is labeled as a "bunch of crooks." *De Mankowski v. Ship Channel Dev. Co.*, 300 S.W. 118, 122 (Tex. Civ. App.—Galveston 1927, no writ).

A plaintiff can be either a private or public plaintiff. This distinction is important for determining the applicable burden of proof (see discussion *infra* § IV(B)(3) for additional information). A plaintiff is private unless the defendant proves it is public. The United States Court of Appeals for the Fifth Circuit has held that a business owner or corporate plaintiff is not a "public figure" in a libel case merely by virtue of its advertising. *Golden Bear Distrib. Sys., Inc. v. Chase Revel, Inc.*, 708 F.2d 944, 952 (5th Cir. 1983) (advertising alone was insufficient to qualify corporation as public figure where corporation had not thrust itself into public controversy). See also *Blue Ridge Bank v. Veribanc, Inc.*, 866 F.2d 681, 686-88 (4th Cir. 1989) (plaintiff bank's advertising was insufficient to qualify bank as public figure where advertising was not related to matter in controversy). However, an opposite conclusion has been reached in the Third Circuit. *Steaks Unlimited, Inc. v. Deaner*, 623 F.2d 264, 273-75 (3d Cir. 1980).

(2) Proper Defendants

Just as the plaintiff must prove it is a proper plaintiff, the plaintiff must also prove that the defendant is a proper defendant. A proper defendant can be an individual and/or an entity. An individual who publishes or republishes a defamatory statement is liable and generally is not excused even when some entity is also liable. An entity is a proper defendant when an officer or agent makes a defamatory statement: (1) while acting within his or her general authority; and (2) for the benefit of the entity. *Minyard Food Stores, Inc. v. Goodman*, 80 S.W.3d 573, 577-78 (Tex. 2002). Neither express authorization nor subsequent ratification is necessary to establish entity liability. *Texam Oil Corp. v. Poynor*, 436 S.W.2d 129, 130 (Tex. 1968).

A defendant can be either a non-media or a media defendant. This distinction is important for the privilege defense. A defendant is non-media unless it is a newspaper or other periodical. See Tex. Civ. Prac. & Rem. Code § 73.002(a).

(3) Definition and Elements

Once the proper plaintiff(s) and proper defendant(s) are identified, the plaintiff must prove a valid cause of action for defamation exists. The plaintiff must prove the following elements:

(1) The defendant made a defamatory statement concerning the plaintiff;

(2) The defendant published or permitted to be published the defamatory statement to a third party;

(3) The publication resulted from intentional or negligent conduct by the defendant; and

(4) Actual damages resulted from the publication or the statement is defamatory per se.

Restatement (Second) of Torts § 558. There are additional requirements if the plaintiff is a public plaintiff—the public plaintiff must prove by clear and convincing evidence that the defendant made false and defamatory statements with actual malice. *New York Times Co. v. Sullivan*, 376 U.S. 254, 279-80, 284 (1964); *Casso v. Brand*, 776 S.W.2d 551, 554 (Tex. 1989); *El Paso Times, Inc. v. Trexler*, 447 S.W.2d 403, 405 (Tex. 1969). A statement is made with actual malice when it is made with knowledge that it is false or with reckless disregard for its truth. *New York Times*, 376 U.S. at 279-80, 284; *Hearst Corp. v. Skeen*, 159 S.W.3d 633, 637 (Tex. 2005). If a qualified privilege is held by the defendant (see discussion *infra* § IV(B)(4)(c)), the private plaintiff must also prove the defendant acted with actual malice. *Randall's Food Mkts. Inc. v. Johnson*, 891 S.W.2d 640, 646 (Tex. 1995).

The foregoing elements apply to the two types of defamation suits—slander and libel. See *Cain v. Heart Corp.*, 878 S.W.2d 577, 580 (Tex. 1994). Slander is oral defamation. *Id.* Libel is written defamation. *Id.* In Texas, common law governs both types, except to the extent that libel actions are limited or extended by Sections 73.001 to 73.006 of the Texas Civil Practice & Remedies Code.

Under Section 73.001, even if the plaintiff proves all the foregoing elements of defamation an action for libel will only be valid if one of the following listed injuries was the result of the defamation:

(1) Exposure to public hatred;
(2) Contempt or ridicule;
(3) Financial injury;
(4) Impeachment of the plaintiff's honesty, integrity, virtue, or reputation; or
(5) Publishing one's natural defects and thereby exposing the person to public hatred, ridicule, or financial injury.

See *Deen v. Snyder,* 57 S.W.2d 338, 340 (Tex. Civ. App.— Fort Worth 1933, no writ); Tex. Civ. Prac. & Rem. Code § 73.001. Finally, the statute of limitations for a libel or slander claim is one-year, which runs from either the date of discovery or from the date of mass publication or communication. Tex. Civ. Prac. & Rem. Code § 16.002; *Kelley v. Rinkle*, 532 S.W.2d 947, 949 (Tex. 1976); *Ross v. Arkwright Mut. Ins. Co.,* 892 S.W.2d 119, 131 (Tex. App.—Houston [14th Dist.] 1994, writ denied); *Langston v. Eagle Publ'g Co.*, 719 S.W.2d 612, 615 (Tex. App.—Waco 1986, writ ref'd n.r.e.).

(a) Statement Must be Defamatory

Whether the statement is defamatory is a question of law for the court. *Turner v. KTRK Television, Inc.*, 38 S.W.3d 103, 114 (Tex. 2000); *Carr v. Brasher*, 776 S.W.2d 567, 569 (Tex. 1989). The court considers the statement as a whole in light of the surrounding circumstances based upon how a person of ordinary intelligence would perceive the entire statement. *Musser v. Smith Protective Servs.,*

Inc., 723 S.W.2d 653, 655 (Tex. 1987); *Hearst,* 130 S.W.3d at 918. A publication can convey a false and defamatory meaning by omitting or juxtaposing facts, even though all the story's individual statements considered in isolation are literally true or non-defamatory. *Turner,* 38 S.W.3d at 115. Only when the court finds that the language is ambiguous or of doubtful meaning should the jury then determine the statement's meaning and the effect the statement's publication has on an ordinary reader. *Musser,* 723 S.W.2d at 655.

(b) Publication to Third Parties

The allegedly defamatory statement must be published to a third person to be actionable. See *Shearson Lehman Hutton v. Tucker,* 806 S.W.2d 914, 921 (Tex. App.—Corpus Christi 1991, writ dism'd w.o.j.). The statement need only be published to one party other than the person allegedly defamed. See *Frank B. Hall & Co. v. Buck,* 678 S.W.2d 612, 617 (Tex. App.—Houston [14th Dist.] 1984, writ ref'd n.r.e), *cert. denied,* 472 U.S. 10009 (1985). Defamatory statements communicated only among fellow employees of a business entity may not be considered "published." See *Walker v. Martin,* 129 S.W.2d 1149, 1151 (Tex. Civ. App.—San Antonio 1939, no writ). But see *Montgomery Ward & Co. v. Peaster,* 178 S.W.2d 302, 305-06 (Tex. Civ. App.—Eastland 1944, no writ) (communication must be between individuals who have a duty with regard to the transaction which is the subject matter of the defamation).

(c) Intentional or Negligent Publication

The publication must result from either the intentional or negligent conduct of the defendant. See *First State Bank v. Ake,* 606 S.W.2d 696, 701 (Tex. Civ.

App.—Corpus Christi 1980, writ ref'd n.r.e.). Intentional publication may occur even though the defendant is mistaken as to the identity of the person to whom he or she publishes the defamatory statement. *Frank B. Hall*, 678 S.W.2d at 617-18. Negligent publication occurs when a reasonable person would recognize that his or her actions will create an unreasonable risk that a defamatory statement will be communicated to a third party. *First State Bank*, 606 S.W.2d at 701.

(d) Actual Damages or Per Se Defamatory

Finally, the plaintiff must prove actual damages were incurred, unless the utterance is defamatory *per se*, then the existence of damages is presumed. See *Leyendecker & Assocs. v. Wechter,* 683 S.W.2d 369, 374 (Tex. 1984); *Houston Belt & Terminal Ry. v. Wherry,* 548 S.W.2d 743, 752-53 (Tex. App.—Houston [1st Dist.] 1976, writ ref'd n.r.e.). If the defendant is a media defendant, a private plaintiff who establishes liability under a negligence standard must also prove actual damages. *Foster v. Laredo Newspapers, Inc.*, 541 S.W.2d 809, 818-20 (Tex. 1976). Defamation is *per se* when the communication constitutes either (1) libel under Section 73.001 and/or (2) the statement (i) asserts the plaintiff committed an act that is generally regarded as involving moral turpitude, or (ii) causes injury to a person's office, business, profession or occupation. *Eidinoff v. Andress,* 321 S.W.2d 368, 369-70 (Tex. Civ. App.—El Paso 159, writ ref'd n.r.e.); *Tatum v. Liner,* 749 S.W.2d 251, 258 (Tex. App.—San Antonio 1988, no writ) (holding that statements that disparage a person's ability to do his or her job, including statements that impute the person's honesty or ethics, are defamatory *per se*). See also *Gulf Const. Co. v. Mott*, 442 S.W.2d 778, 784 (Tex. Civ.

App.—Houston [14th Dist.] 1969, no writ) (holding that statements that the plaintiff was not creditworthy were defamatory *per se*); *Shearson Lehman Hutton*, 806 S.W.2d at 921 (statements made about former employee that he would lose his stockbroker's license, was in trouble with the SEC, and would never work as a stockbroker again were deemed slanderous *per se*).

(4) Privileges

Even if all the elements of defamation are proven, a privilege can be asserted to bar liability. Privileges are affirmative defenses that must be plead and proven by the defendant in a defamation action. In Texas, privileges can be separated into two categories: (1) those available to media defendants under Texas Civil Practice and Remedies Code Section 73.002; and (2) those available to all defendants under the common law.

(a) Section 73.002 Privilege

Section 73.002 of the Texas Civil Practice and Remedies Code provides a privilege for publications by newspapers or periodicals regarding certain public events or matters of public concern. To the extent the statutory privilege applies, any fair, true and impartial account of any proceeding or statement made during any proceeding listed in Texas Civil Practice and Remedies Code 73.002(b) is privileged and may not serve as the basis of a libel action against a media defendant. See *Humane Society of Dallas v. Dallas Morning News, L.P.*, 180 S.W.3d 921 (Tex. App.—Dallas 2005, no pet. h.). The list of proceedings includes the following: (1) judicial proceedings; (2) official proceedings to administer the law; (3) executive or legislative proceedings; and (4) proceedings of a public meeting dealing with a public purpose. Tex. Civ. Prac. & Rem. Code § 73.002(b). However, this privilege is lost if the defendant published the defamatory matter with actual malice. *Langston,* 719 S.W.2d at 624.

(b) Common-Law Absolute Privilege

Texas common law provides privileges for all defendants (not just newspapers and periodicals). There are two broad categories of common-law privileges: absolute and qualified. *Hearst,* 103 S.W.2d at 926. These privileges may be waived if the defamation is "republished." *Id.*

An absolute privilege means the defendant cannot be liable for defamation, regardless of the falsity of the statement or the malice with which the statements are made. *Reagan v. Guardian Life Ins. Co.,* 166 S.W.2d 909, 912 (Tex. 1942). An absolute privilege applies to statements made during judicial, quasi-judicial and legislative hearings. *Hurlbut v. Gulf Atlantic Life Ins. Co.,* 749 S.W.2d 762, 768 (Tex. 1987); *Daystar Residential, Inc. v. Collmar,* 176 W.W. 3d 24, 27-28 (Tex. App. —Houston [13th Dist.] 2004, pet. denied). The absolute privilege has also been extended to the filing of a *lis pendens. Sharif-Munir-Davidson Dev. Corp. v. Bell,* 788 S.W.2d 427, 430 (Tex. App.—Dallas 1990, writ denied). Texas courts are divided as to whether the absolute privilege applies when the remarks are irrelevant to the proceeding. See *Gaither v. Davis,* 582 S.W.2d 913, 913-14 (Tex. Civ. App.—Fort Worth 1979, writ dism'd w.o.j.) and *Butler v. Lilly,* 533 S.W.2d 130, 133-35 (Tex. Civ. App.—Houston [1st Dist.] 1976, writ dism'd w.o.j.) (finding that communications in the course of a judicial proceeding are absolutely privileged whether or not they are relevant in the context of the proceeding). Compare *Jenevein v. Friedman,* 114 S.W.3d 743, 745-49 (Tex. App.—Dallas 2003, pet. filed); *Bennett v. Computer Assoc. Int'l,* 932 S.W.2d 197, 201 (Tex. App.—Amarillo 1996, writ denied) (noting that to be privileged, the statement must bear some relation to proposed or existing litigation). The defendant must prove that the statements were accurately reported to prove the privilege applies. *Scripps Texas Newspapers, LP v. Belalcazar,* 99 S.W.3d 829, 836-37 (Tex. App.—Corpus Christi 2003, pet denied).

Examples of statements made during quasi-judicial hearings that have been found to be absolutely privileged include statements made to the Texas Board of Medical Examiners (TBME) and the Federal Aviation Administration (FAA). See *Ramires v. Tex. State Bd. of Med. Exam'rs,* 927 S.W.2d 770, 773 (Tex. App.—Austin 1996, pet. denied); *5-State Helicopters, Inc. v. Cox,* 146 S.W.3d 254, 256-60 (Tex. App.—Fort Worth July 29, 2004, pet. denied). However, to remain absolutely privileged, such statements must call upon the agency to investigate, exercise judgment, or impose penalties. See *Stephan v. Baylor Med. Ctr.,* 20 S.W.3d 880, 890 (Tex. App.—Dallas 2000, pet. denied).

(c) Common-Law Qualified Privilege

Unlike absolute privileges, qualified privileges are lost if the defamatory statement was made with actual malice. See *Gillum v. Republic Health Corp.,* 778 S.W.2d 558, 572 (Tex. App.—Dallas 1989, no writ). Qualified privileges exist under circumstances "where a person having a common interest in a particular subject matter may reasonably believe that facts exist which another,

sharing that common interest, is entitled to know." *Id.*;
Marathon Oil Co. v. Salazar, 682 S.W.2d 624, 630 (Tex.
App.—Houston [1st Dist.] 1984, writ ref'd n.r.e.). The
following are circumstance under which courts have
examined whether a qualified privilege attaches to a
business communication:

(1)   Statements made while investigating
an incident regarding an employee. *Austin v.
Inet Tech., Inc.,* 118 S.W.3d 491, 494-98 (Tex.
App.—Dallas 2003, no pet.);

(2)   Internal investigation of an employee's
alleged misconduct. *Randall's Food Mkt., Inc.,*
891 S.W.2d at 646-48;

(3)   Statements made in connection with an
employer's evaluation of an employee's job performance. *Boze v. Branstetter*, 912 F.2d 801, 806
(5th Cir. 1990);

(4)   Better Business Bureau's communications
to its members regarding plaintiff's solicitation
techniques. *Assoc. Tel. Directory Publishers,
Inc. v. Better Bus. Bureau, Inc.*, 710 S.W.2d 190,
191 (Tex. App.—Corpus Christi 1986, writ ref'd
n.r.e.);

(5)   Employer's accusations of an
employee's misconduct in the workplace. *Marathon Oil*, 682 S.W.2d at 630-31;

(6)   A complaint by a drug manufacturer to the
State Board of Pharmacy regarding a pharmacist's

license. *Bloom v. A. H. Robins Co.*, 479 S.W.2d 780, 781-82 (Tex. Civ. App.—Waco 1972, writ ref'd n.r.e.), *cert. denied*, 410 U.S. 983 (1973);

(7)   A credit report by a credit agency. *O'Neil v. Dun & Bradstreet, Inc.*, 448 S.W.2d 153, 154-58 (Tex. Civ. App.—El Paso 1969), *rev'd on other grounds*, 456 S.W.2d 896 (Tex. 1970);

(8)   A report to the State Life Insurance Commissioner of the termination of a life insurance agent. *Thornton v. Rio Grande Nat'l Life Ins. Co.*, 367 S.W.2d 950, 951-52 (Tex. Civ. App.—Waco 1963, writ ref'd n.r.e.); and

(9)   Charges of fraud made against a minister during a church disciplinary proceeding and distributed to church members. *Browning v. Gomez*, 332 S.W.2d 588, 591-92 (Tex. Civ. App.—Austin 1960, writ ref'd n.r.e.).

(5) Remedies

Once the plaintiff has proved the elements of defamation and it is established that no privilege exits, damages are imposed. There are three types of recoverable damages: actual, special, and exemplary.

(a) Actual/General Damages

General damages are those that necessarily and directly result from the defamation. *Bolling v. Baker,* 671 S.W.2d 559, 569 (Tex. App.—San Antonio 1984, writ dism'd w.o.j.). These damages are presumed as a matter of law and "are recoverable under a general averment without proof that they have been incurred." *Id.* When a corporation suffers damages as a direct and proximate result of the defamation, evidence concerning the extent of the injury is a proper matter for the jury's consideration. *British Overseas Airways Corp. v. Tours and Travel, Inc.,* 568 S.W.2d 888, 894 (Tex. Civ. App.—Houston [1st Dist.] 1978, writ ref'd n.r.e.). When an individual suffers damages, injuries to character or reputation, feelings, mental anguish, and other similar wrongs incapable of money valuation are recoverable. *Vista Chevrolet, Inc. v. Barron,* 698 S.W.2d 435, 441 (Tex. App.—Corpus Christi 1985, no writ). Individual recovery for actual damages for mental anguish requires more than mere worry or anxiety—the plaintiff must prove "intense pain of body or mind, or a high degree of mental suffering." *Ryder Truck Rentals v. Latham,* 593 S.W.2d 334, 339 (Tex. Civ. App.—El Paso 1979, writ ref'd n.r.e.).

(b) Special Damages

Damages that are not general are special; they must be foreseeable to the defendant but are not a necessary and usual result of the wrong. See *Arthur Andersen & Co. v. Perry Equip. Corp.,* 945 S.W.2d 812, 816 (Tex. 1997). Special damages are only required to be proved for recovery, if, the defamatory words are such that they would not affect a person in one type of business more than they would affect a person in any other type of business. See *Brough v. Enyart,* 658 S.W.2d 221, 226 (Tex. App.—Corpus Christi 1983, writ ref'd n.r.e.). Lost profits is one type of recoverable special damage. Lost profits may be recovered when:

> it is shown that a loss of profits is the natural and probable consequence[ ] of the

> act or omission complained of, and their amount is shown with sufficient certainty...It is not necessary that profits should be susceptible of exact calculation, it is sufficient that there be data from which they may be ascertained with a reasonable degree of certainty and exactness.

Texas Instruments, Inc. v. Teletron Energy Mgmt., Inc., 877 S.W.2d 276, 279 (Tex.1994). In calculating lost profits, a company's profits are compared before and after the alleged defamatory statement. See *British Overseas Airways,* 568 S.W.2d at 894. In the case of a newly established business, lost profits are not as easily calculated and are not always available. *Golden Bear Distrib. Sys.,* 708 F.2d at 950-51. In *Golden Bear,* the court concluded that sufficient evidence existed to award lost profits and reasoned that the record for profitability, rather than the age of the business, determines whether lost profits are recoverable. *Id.* at 951. However, new businesses often cannot recover lost profits because "the profits which might have been made from such businesses are not susceptible of being established by proof to that degree of certainty which the law demands." *Texas Instruments, Inc.,* 877 S.W.2d at 280.

Loss of time damages are composed of two elements: time and rate. *Vista Chevrolet,* 698 S.W.2d at 440-42. The jury must be instructed that "loss of time" means "loss of earnings" which is different from "decreased earning capacity." *Id.* A jury instruction on decreased earning capacity would not be duplicative of an instruction on loss of time or loss of earnings. *Id.* As for an individual plaintiff, special damages include damages for sickness or

Civil Action No. 2-97-398 (N.D. Tex.)); Texturf 10 grass being portrayed negatively by an agronomist (*Anderton v. McAfee*, Cause No. 96-12667 (134th Jud. Dist. Ct. Dallas County, Texas); and another case against Winfrey regarding "Mad Cow Disease"(*Cactus Feeding Club, Inc. v. Winfrey*, No. 2:98-CV-00151 (N.D. Tex. 1998)).

(2) The Texas Deceptive Trade Practices Act

The Texas Deceptive Trade Practices Act provides a "laundry list" of violations including "disparaging the goods, services, or business of another by a false or misleading representation of facts." Tex. Bus. & Com. Code § 17.46 (b)(8). If this act is violated, a plaintiff can recover punitive damages for a "knowing" violation of the statute and attorney's fees.

V. FRAUD

A. Introduction

B. Definition and Elements

    (1) Material Misrepresentation

    (2) Falsity

    (3) Knowledge

    (4) Intent to Induce Action

    (5) Reliance

    (6) Causation

C. Fraud Distinguished from a Breach of Contract

D. Examples

E. Damages

F. Selected Defenses

    (1) Waiver or Ratification

    (2) Estoppel and Quasi-estoppel

    (3) Statute of Limitations

A. Introduction

Fraud is a recognized cause of action under both Texas common law and Texas statutory law. Generally, fraud consists of "an act, omission, or concealment in the breach of a legal duty, trust, or confidence justly imposed, where the breach causes injury to another or the taking of undue advantage." 41 Tex. Jur. 3d *Fraud and Deceit* § 1 (1998).

B. Definition and Elements

The elements of common-law fraud are: (1) a material misrepresentation; (2) which was false; (3) known to be false when made or asserted without knowledge of the truth; (4) intended to be acted upon; (5) relied upon by plaintiff; and (6) caused injury. *Johnson & Higgins of Texas, Inc. v. Kenneco Energy, Inc.*, 962 S.W.2d 507, 524 (Tex. 1998); *Ernst & Young,L.L.P. v. Pac. Mut. Life Ins. Co.*, 51 S.W.3d 573, 577 (Tex. 2001). Common-law fraud encompasses both actual and constructive fraud. Actual fraud usually occurs when one party operates with an intent to deceive. See *Flanary v. Mills*, 150 S.W.3d 785, 795 (Tex. App.—Austin 2004, no pet.). Constructive fraud involves "those breaches that the law condemns as 'fraudulent' merely because they tend to deceive others, violate confidences, or cause injury to public interests, regardless of the actor's mental state." *Id.*

Under the Texas Business and Commerce Code, a cause of action for fraud exists in transactions involving real estate or stock in a corporation or a joint stock company. Tex. Bus. & Com. Code Ann. § 27.01 (Vernon 2002). Two types of statutory fraud can be alleged under this statute. First, a cause of action can consist of a false representation of a past or existing material fact, when the false representation is made to a person for the purpose of inducing that person to enter into a contract and the misrepresentation is actually relied on in entering the contract. *Id.* at § 27.01(a)(1). The second type of fraud consists of a false promise to do an act. The false promise must be: (1) material; (2) made with the intention of not fulfilling it; (3) made to a person for the purpose of inducing such person to enter into a contract; and (4) relied on in entering into the contract. *Id.* at § 27.01(a)(2).

The difference between fraud at common law and statutory fraud is that common-law fraud does not require knowledge of the falseness of the representation when actual damages are sought. See *Swanson v. Schlumberger Tech. Corp.*, 895 S.W.2d 719, 732 (Tex. App.—Texarkana 1994, no writ). Statutory fraud, on the other hand, allows for exemplary damages only if the defendant had actual knowledge of the falsity of the statement when it was made. Tex. Bus. & Com. Code Ann. § 27.01(c). Other than the knowledge requirement in an exemplary damages situation, the elements are substantially the same and are examined below.

(1) Material Misrepresentation

A misrepresentation has been defined under Texas law as: (1) a false statement of fact; (2) a promise of future performance made with intent to not perform; (3)

a statement of opinion based on a false statement of fact; or (4) an expression of opinion that is false, made by one claiming or implying to have special knowledge of the subject matter of the opinion. See *Tilton v. Marshall*, 925 S.W.2d 672, 685-86 (Tex. 1996). A misrepresentation is material if it is important to the defrauded party in making a decision. *Cohn v. Comm'n for Lawyer Discipline*, 979 S.W.2d 694, 698 (Tex. App.—Houston [14th Dist.] 1998, no pet.). That is, materiality "'means a reasonable person would attach importance to and would be induced to act on the information in determining his choice of actions in the transaction in question.'" *Id.* (quoting *Beneficial Personnel) Serv. v. Porras,* 927 S.W.2d 177, 186 (Tex. App.—El Paso 1996)). An action in fraud cannot be based on an opinion, but must be based on a factual misrepresentation. See *Transp. Ins. Co. v. Faircloth*, 898 S.W.2d 269, 276 (Tex. 1995). However, when the speaker knows the opinion is false, a fraud claim is appropriate. See *Tex. Indus. Trust, Inc. v. Luck,* 312 S.W.2d 324, 327 (Tex. Civ. App.—San Antonio 1958, writ ref'd).

The omission of a material fact cannot give rise to fraud unless there is a duty to disclose, which can be based on: (1) an agreement of the parties; (2) a confidential relationship; (3) a partial disclosure when the failure to disclose the complete facts creates a false impression; or (4) a situation where the speaker has made a statement that the speaker knows the other is relying on, learns new information that makes the prior statement untrue or misleading, and fails to correct the prior false or misleading statement. See *Trs. of the N.W. Laundry & Dry Cleaners Health & Welfare Trust Fund v. Burzynski*, 27 F.3d 153, 157 (5th Cir. 1994).

(2) Falsity

The material representation upon which a fraud action is based must be false. Falsity is determined at the time the representation is made and cannot be based upon a statement that later becomes false. See *Trenholm v. Ratcliff*, 646 S.W.2d 927, 930 (Tex. 1983). Even if a statement is literally true, it can satisfy the element of falsity if it used to create a false impression. *Blanton v. Sherman Compress Co.*, 256 S.W.2d 884, 886-87 (Tex. Civ. App.—Dallas 1953, no writ) (statement by defendant that he had talked with his father, although true, was used to mislead plaintiff about whether or not defendant's father had explicitly given permission).

(3) Knowledge

A material misrepresentation must be made knowingly. To maintain an action for fraud, the plaintiff must prove that the defendant knew that the statement was false or made a positive assertion with reckless disregard for the validity of the statement. See *Trenholm*, 646 S.W.2d at 930.

(4) Intent to Induce Action

Not only must the material misrepresentation be made knowingly, but it must also be made with the intent to induce action. See *Sears, Roebuck & Co. v. Meadows*, 877 S.W.2d 281, 282 (Tex. 1994). The plaintiff must show that he or she is the person from which the speaker intended to induce action. See *Jefmor, Inc. v. Chicago Title Ins. Co.*, 839 S.W.2d 161, 164 (Tex. App.—Fort Worth 1992, no writ). The intent of the speaker in a fraud claim requires proof of a greater degree of purposeful conduct than that required under a foreseeability standard. *Blue Bell, Inc. v. Peat, Marwick, Mitchell & Co.*, 715 S.W.2d 408, 415 (Tex. App.—Dallas 1986, writ ref'd n.r.e.) (noting the fact that "it *should be* known that another will rely upon a misrepresentation does not, of itself, establish that the misrepresentation was made with the *intent* to induce reliance").

(5) Reliance

A plaintiff must show reliance to its detriment upon the material misrepresentation. Such reliance must be justifiable under the circumstances. *Gen. Motors Corp., Pontiac Motor Div. v. Courtesy Pontiac, Inc.*, 538 S.W.2d 3, 6 (Tex. Civ. App.—Tyler 1976, no writ). A person's intelligence, experience, and education may be examined as well as the facts and circumstances at the time of the supposedly fraudulent transaction to determine whether or not reliance was justifiable. See *id.*

(6) Causation

To prevail on a cause of action for fraud, the plaintiff must show that a loss occurred as a result of the fraudulent transaction. *Travelers Ins. Co. v. Delta Air Lines, Inc.*, 498 S.W.2d 443, 447 (Tex. Civ. App.—Texarkana 1973, no writ). That is, there must be a causal connection that is directly traceable to the material misrepresentation. See *id.*

C. Fraud Distinguished from a Breach of Contract

Texas courts have explained the distinction between a cause of action for fraud as opposed to a cause of action for a breach of contract. However, prior to the distinction, there existed a difficulty in determining whether the failure to perform under a contract gave rise to an action in tort in addition to an action for breach of contract. Although it is now well settled that failure to perform the terms of a contract is not typically a tort, when one party enters into a contract with no intention of performing, that misrepresentation may give rise to a claim of fraud. See *Crim Truck & Tractor Co. v. Navistar Int'l Transp. Corp.*, 823 S.W.2d 591, 597 (Tex. 1992).

D. Examples

(1) Plaintiff shareholder in construction company prevailed on claim for common-law fraud where partner breached fiduciary duty by not disclosing actual profits of company and under compensating plaintiff for plaintiff's share of profits. *Flanary v. Mills*, 150 S.W.3d 785, 795-796 (Tex. App.—Austin 2004, no pet.).

(2) Plaintiff contractor's claim for fraud failed where plaintiff could not prove statement that "as long as you do your job, you'll have a job" was untrue when statement was made to plaintiff. *Airborne Freight Corp., Inc. v. C.R. Lee Enters., Inc.*, 847 S.W.2d 289, 297 (Tex. App.—El Paso 1992, writ denied).

(3) Plaintiff tenant failed on claim of statutory fraud because reliance on allegedly fraudulent warranties and representations was unreasonable due to presence of "as is" provision in commercial lease. See *Gym-N-I Playgrounds, Inc. v. Snider*, 158 S.W.3d 78, 88 (Tex. App.—Austin 2005, pet. filed).

(4) Plaintiff real estate broker was able to maintain an action for fraud when prospective purchaser entered agreement with no intent to perform under the agreement. *Markman v. Gaitz*, 499 S.W.2d 692, 697 (Tex. Civ. App.—Houston [1st Dist.] 1973, writ ref'd n.r.e.).

E. Damages

There are generally three measures of damages available to a plaintiff in an action for fraud. The first available measure of damages is "out-of-pocket" damages. This measure allows a plaintiff to recover the difference between what the plaintiff parted with and what he or she received in reliance on fraudulent representations. See *Airborne Freight*, 847 S.W.2d at 295.

The second measure of damages available to a plaintiff is the "benefit of the bargain." The plaintiff can recover the difference between the value as represented and the actual value received. See *Leyendecker & Assocs., Inc. v. Wechter*, 683 S.W.2d 369, 373 (Tex. 1984).

Finally, in the proper case a plaintiff can recover consequential or special damages. See *Formosa Plastics Corp. USA v. Presidio Engr's and Contractors, Inc.*, 960 S.W.2d 41, 49 n.1 (Tex. 1998). These damages must be pled and proved as proximately resulting from the acts of the defendant. See *Airborne Freight*, 847 S.W.2d at 295. For special damages to be awarded, actual damage must have occurred, and the fraud must be committed willfully, i.e., the speaker must have known that the representation was untrue when made. *Griffin v. Phillips*, 542 S.W.2d 432, 434 (Tex.

Civ. App.—Eastland 1976, writ ref'd n.r.e.). The Texas Supreme Court has recognized that in the proper case "consequential damages could include foreseeable profits from other business opportunities lost as a result of the fraudulent representation." *Formosa Plastics Corp.,* 960 S.W.2d at 49 n.1.

F. Selected Defenses

(1) Waiver or Ratification

A claim for fraud can be waived and/or ratified. A party whose actions affirm a contract induced by fraud may waive a claim for fraud if the party's actions "are done with full knowledge of the fraud and of all material facts, and with the intention clearly manifested of abiding by the contract and waiving all right to recover for the deception." *Viracola v. Dallas Int'l Bank*, 508 S.W.2d 472, 474-75 (Tex. Civ. App.—Waco 1974, writ ref'd n.r.e.).

(2) Estoppel and Quasi-estoppel

The defense of estoppel arises where one party has caused another party to detrimentally change position. *Vessels v. Anschutz Corp.*, 823 S.W.2d 762, 765 (Tex. App.—Texarkana 1992, writ denied). Quasi-estoppel prevents a party from changing position to another party's disadvantage. *Id.* Quasi-estoppel "applies when it would be unconscionable to allow a person to maintain a position inconsistent with one in which he acquiesced, or of which he accepted a benefit." *Id.* at 765-66.

(3) Statute of Limitations

A four-year statute of limitations exists for a fraud action. Tex. Civ. Prac. & Rem. Code Ann. § 16.004 (a)(4)(Vernon 2002); see also *Boulle v. Boulle*, 160 S.W.3d 167, 175 (Tex. App.—Dallas 2005, pet. denied). The statute of limitations begins to run "when a wrongful act causes some legal injury, even if the fact of injury is not discovered until later, and even if all resulting damages have not yet occurred." *Boulle*, 160 S.W.3d at 175.

VI. MISAPPROPRIATION OF TRADE SECRETS AND IMPROPER USE OF CONFIDENTIAL INFORMATION

A. Introduction

B. Serving the Public Interest by Protecting Trade Secrets

C. Definition and Elements

    (1) Existence of a Trade Secret

    (2) Discovery of Secret by Improper Means

    (3) Breach of Confidential Relationship

D. Defenses

    (1) Statute of Limitations as a Defense

    (2) Later Public Disclosure as a Defense

        (a) Disclosure Through Patenting

        (b) Limited Disclosure

E. The Employment Relationship

F. The Inevitable Disclosure Doctrine

G. Injunctive Relief

H. Damages

    (1) Actual Damages

    (2) Exemplary/Punitive Damages

I. Other Possible Causes of Action
    (1) Breach of Covenants Not to Compete
    (2) Breach of Non-Disclosure and Confidentiality
         Agreements
    (3) Breach of Duty of Loyalty
    (4) Computer Fraud and Abuse Act
    (5) Criminal Liability

A. Introduction

The United States Supreme Court has specifically recognized that neither the patent clause of the United States Constitution nor the federal patent laws preempt the legitimate interest of state law in protecting business and trade secrets. *Kewanee Oil Co. v. Bicron Corp.*, 416 U.S. 470 (1974). Texas courts have traditionally recognized the tort of misappropriation of trade secrets and often employ the phrase "use of confidential information" to denote the same action.[1] The tort has

---

[1]   Although many use the terms "trade secret" and "confidential information" synonymously, there is a difference. As the Restatement has long recognized, information may be confidential even if it is not a trade secret. Restatement (Second) of Torts § 757 cmt. b (1939). Accordingly, it may be possible for liability to arise from breach of a confidential relationship where a trade secret is not involved. See *Stewart & Stevenson Servs., Inc. v. Serv-Tech, Inc.*, 879 S.W.2d 89, 96 (Tex. App.—Houston [14th Dist.] 1994, writ denied). It is not, however, possible to have a cause of action for misappropriation of confidential information. *Id.* If an employee discloses confidential information in violation of a confidentiality agreement, however, the employee may be liable for breach of that agreement regardless of whether the information is a trade secret. See *Simplified Telesys, Inc. v. Live Oak Telecom, L.L.C.*, 68 S.W.3d 688, 693 (Tex. App.—Austin 2000, pet. denied); see also *Trilogy Software, Inc. v. Callidus Software, Inc.*, 143 S.W.3d 452, 468 (Tex. App.—Austin 2004, pet. denied).

expanded beyond the traditional fields of inventions and mechanical devices to areas of business knowledge less capable of specific definitions.

B. Serving the Public Interest by Protecting Trade Secrets

As early as 1958, in *Hyde Corp. v. Huffines*, 314 S.W.2d 763 (Tex. 1958), the Texas Supreme Court recognized and encouraged the trend toward protecting trade secrets. In discussing the effect of an injunction upon a defendant charged civilly with the theft of a trade secret, the court noted:

> when . . . a choice must be made between the possible punitive operation of the writ and the failure to provide adequate protection of a recognized legal right, the latter course seems indicated and the undoubted tendency of the law has been to recognize and enforce higher standards of commercial morality in the business world.

Hyde Corp., 314 S.W.2d at 773.

Courts recognize that the public interest is served by protecting trade secrets. *Picker Int'l, Inc. v. Blanton*, 756 F. Supp. 971, 983 (N.D. Tex. 1990). In *Metallurgical Indus., Inc. v. Fourtek*, 790 F.2d 1195, 1201 (5th Cir. 1986), the court stated that the equitable underpinnings of trade secret law are demonstrated by the fact that the cost of devising the secret and the value the secret provides are the criteria in the legal formulation of a trade secret. It seems only fair that one should be able to keep and enjoy the fruits of his or her work. "If a businessman has worked hard, has used his imagination, and has taken bold steps to gain an advantage over his competitors, he should be able to profit from his efforts." *Id.* Because a commercial advantage can disappear once the competition learns of it, the law protects the businessperson's efforts to keep the achievements secret. *Id.*

C. Definition and Elements

In Texas, the common-law tort of misappropriation of trade secrets has the following four elements: (1) the existence of a trade secret; (2) the trade secret was acquired through a confidential relationship or through improper means; (3) the trade secret was used or disclosed without the owner's authorization; and (4) damages resulted from the misappropriation. See *General Universal Sys. v. Lee*, 379 F.3d 131, 149 (5th Cir. 2004); see also *Taco Cabana Int'l, Inc. v. Two Pesos, Inc.*, 932 F.2d 1113, 1123 (5th Cir. 1991); see also *Avera v. Clark Moulding*, 791 S.W.2d 144, 145 (Tex. App.—Dallas 1990, no writ).

(1) Existence of a Trade Secret

A trade secret is any formula, pattern, device, or compilation of information used in one's business, and which gives an opportunity to obtain an advantage over competitors who do not know or use it. See *Taco Cabana*, 932 F.2d at 1123; *Hyde Corp.*, 314 S.W.2d at 776 (adopting Restatement (Second) of Torts § 757 (1939));

see also *Computer Assocs. Int'l, Inc. v. Altai, Inc.,* 918 S.W.2d 453, 455 (Tex. 1996).

In determining whether a trade secret exists, Texas courts look at the following factors:

(1) the extent to which the information is known outside the employer's business;

(2) the extent to which the information is known by employees and others involved in the business;

(3) the extent of the measures taken to guard the secrecy of the information;

(4) the value of the information to the business and its competitors;

(5) the amount of effort exerted in developing the information; and

(6) the ease or difficulty with which the information could be properly acquired or duplicated by others.

Restatement (Second) of Torts § 757 cmt. b (1937); see *Chapa v. Garcia,* 848 S.W.2d 667, 669 (Tex. 1993); see also *In re Bass,* 113 S.W.3d 735, 739 (Tex. 2003); see also *John Paul Mitchell Sys., Inc. v. Randalls Food Mkts., Inc.,* 17 S.W.3d 721, 738 (Tex. App.—Austin 2000, pet. denied). These factors must be weighed in the context of the circumstances, and a party seeking trade secret protection need not satisfy all six factors. In re *Bass,* 113 S.W.3d at 740.

Additionally, a person's subjective belief that there is a secret suggests that the secret exists. A manufacturer presumably would not incur costs for security measures if it believed its competitors already knew the very information the manufacturer sought to protect. *Fourtek*, 790 F.2d at 1199.

It is error to consider novelty and uniqueness as conditions precedent to the existence of a trade secret. *Gonzales v. Zamora*, 791 S.W.2d 258, 263-64 (Tex. App.—Corpus Christi 1990, no writ). Indeed, the "scope of protectable trade secrets is far broader than the scope of patentable technology." *CVD, Inc. v. Raytheon*, 769 F.2d 842, 850 (1st Cir. 1985); see also *FMC Corp. v. Varco Int'l, Inc.*, 677 F.2d 500, 502 (5th Cir. 1982); see also *Sikes v. McGraw-Edison Co.*, 665 F.2d 731, 733 (5th Cir. 1982). "[A] trade secret can exist in a combination of characteristics and components, each of which, by itself, is in the public domain, but the united process, design and operation of which is unique combination affords a 'competitive advantage and is a protectable secret.'" *Sikes*, 665 F.2d at 736 (quoting *Imperial Chem. Indus., Ltd. v. Nat'l Distillers & Chem. Corp.*, 342 F.2d 737, 742 (2d Cir. 1965)). "That the scientific principles involved are generally known does not necessarily refute [the plaintiff's] claims of trade secrets." *Fourtek*, 790 F.2d at 1199.

As the above factors (and common sense) would indicate, for something to be a trade secret, it must be a secret or at least have a "substantial element of secrecy." *Rugen v. Interactive Bus. Sys., Inc.*, 864 S.W.2d 548, 549 (Tex. Civ. App.—Dallas 1993, no writ); *Am. Precision Vibrator Co. v. Nat'l Air Vibrator Co.*, 764 S.W.2d 274, 276 (Tex. App.—Houston [1st Dist.] 1988, no writ). "The word secret implies the information is not generally known or readily available. . . However, when money

83

and time are invested in the development of a procedure or device which is based on an idea which is not new to a particular industry, and when that certain procedure or device is not generally known, trade secret protection will exist." *Gonzales*, 791 S.W.2d at 264. "A device or business method that is simple and the construction of which [is] ascertainable at a glance" is not a trade secret. *K & G Oil Tool & Serv. Co. v. G & G Fishing Tool Serv.*, 314 S.W.2d 782, 788 (Tex. 1958). Architectural plans and kitchen layout and design drawings may be trade secrets. See, e.g., *Taco Cabana*, 932 F.2d at 1123.

Customer lists are often a source of trade secret litigation. Customer lists may be protected when the identities or other information about the customers in them is not publicly available. See *Miller Paper Co. v. Roberts Paper Co.*, 901 S.W.2d 593, 601-03 (Tex. App.—Amarillo 1995, no writ); see also *Rugen*, 864 S.W.2d at 551; see also *Am. Precision Vibrator Co.*, 764 S.W.2d at 274; see also *Zoecon Indus. v. Am. Stockman Tag Co.*, 713 F.2d 1174, 1179 (5th Cir. 1983); see also *Fox v. Tropical Warehouses, Inc.*, 121 S.W.3d 853, 859 (Tex. App. Fort Worth 2003, no pet.). However, a customer list of readily ascertainable names and addresses ordinarily will not be protected as a trade secret. *Zoecon Indus.*, 713 F.2d at 1179.

Is there a cause of action for misappropriation of technical information that is not a trade secret? The court said no in *Stuart & Stevenson, Servs., Inc.*, 879 S.W.2d at 99. In rejecting the argument that there could be a claim for "misappropriation of non-secret confidential information," the court concluded: "[f]From all these cases we conclude that there is no cause of action for misappropriation of confidential information that is not either secret or, at least, substantially secret." *Stuart & Stevenson, Servs., Inc.*, 879 S.W.2d at 99. However, this conclusion seemingly contradicts the decision in *U. S. Sporting Prods. v. Johnny Stewart*, 865 S.W.2d 214 (Tex. App.—Waco 1993, writ denied); see *infra* Section IV.B. (Misappropriation as a form of Unfair Competition).

A trade secret is defined not by the type of information, but by the manner in which the information is treated. Accordingly, what constitutes a trade secret will vary from case to case. Indeed, whether the information is a trade secret may be the most contested issue in trade secret disputes. However, once established, courts will protect trade secrets from being improperly disclosed. *Zep Mfg. Co. v. Harthcock*, 824 S.W.2d 654, 663 (Tex. App.— Dallas 1999, no pet.).

(2) Discovery of Secret by Improper Means

Although the existence of this element could satisfy the second element of the tort, in fact, most reported cases involve an alleged breach of a confidential relationship (as discussed below), established through an employer-employee relationship. Nevertheless, a jury finding of the use of improper means to obtain the secret information would suffice; e.g., an actual physical intrusion by a competitor.

In *Jeter v. Assoc. Rack Corp.*, 607 S.W.2d 272 (Tex. Civ. App.—Texarkana 1980, writ ref'd n.r.e.), the court specifically noted that the existence of a lawful means of acquiring confidential material does not excuse the exercise of unlawful means. In *Miller Paper*, the Court noted that information can and should be treated as confidential and protected if the information was obtained wrongfully by an employee, even if it could be obtained through other means. *Miller Paper*, 901 S.W.2d at 601 (n.3).

(3) Breach of Confidential Relationship

In order to prevail on a claim of misappropriation of trade secrets, a plaintiff can establish the second element by proving there was a breach of a confidential relationship. See *Plains Cotton Coop. Ass'n v. Good Pasture Computer Serv., Inc.*, 807 F.2d 1256, 1262 (5th Cir. 1987); see also *Taco Cabana Int'l, Inc.*, 932 F.2d at 1123; see also *Avera*, 791 S.W.2d at 145. It is not necessary that there be an express confidentiality agreement between the employer and employee for material to be confidential or secret. See also *Mercer v. C. A. Roberts Co.*, 570 F.2d 1232, 1238 (5th Cir. 1978); see also *Hyde Corp.*, 314 S.W.2d at 766; see also *Thermotics, Inc. v. Bat-Jac Tool Co.,* 541 S.W.2d 255 (Tex. Civ. App.—Houston [1st Dist.] 1976, no writ). If, however, such an agreement exists, the employer can bring an additional cause of action for breach of contract and, if successful, recover its attorney's fees. Tex. Civ. Prac. & Rem. Code Ann. §§ 38.001-38.003 (Vernon 2005).

Nevertheless, the employee must either have been informed that the information was to have been kept secret or the circumstances must be such that the employee should have known that the material was confidential. In other words, while an express agreement as to non-disclosure of confidential information is not necessary, "the owner of a trade secret must do something to protect itself from the use of such secret. The owner will lose his secret by his disclosure unless in some manner he creates a duty and places that duty upon another not to disclose or use such secret." *Rimes v. Club Corp.*, 542 S.W.2d 909, 913 (Tex. Civ. App.—Dallas 1976, writ ref'd n.r.e.); see also *Am. Precision Vibrator Co.*, 764 S.W.2d at 276. To strengthen proprietary protection, the employer should specifically inform employees in writing as to confidential information and as to company rules against disclosure, as well as limiting the number of employees with access to the information. *Auto Wax Co. v. Byrd*, 599 S.W.2d 110, 112 (Tex. Civ. App.—Dallas 1980, no writ). Additionally, the employer must avoid disclosure of the information through its business practices because public disclosure ordinarily eliminates the secret nature of the information. *Rimes*, 542 S.W.2d at 913. It is the breach of confidence at the time of disclosure that satisfies this element of the tort, and not the motivation of the defendant at the time he enters into the confidential relationship. *Hyde,* 314 S.W.2d at 770.

Of course, as with other torts, the plaintiff must establish that the defendant's use or disclosure of the trade secrets without authorization caused the plaintiff injury. As one would expect, this element is the least litigated.

D. Defenses

(1) Statute of Limitations as a Defense

A three-year statute of limitations applies to misappropriation of trade secrets claims. Tex. Civ. Prac. & Rem. Code § 16.010 (Vernon 2005). Additionally, the discovery rule applies to such actions. See *Computer Assocs.*, 918 S.W.2d at 458-59.

(2) Later Public Disclosure as a Defense

(a) Disclosure Through Patenting

Some uncertainty exists under Texas law as to whether a valid cause of action exists for misappropriation of trade secrets when the information is a trade secret on which a United States patent is later obtained. In *Luccous v. J. C. Kinley Co.*, 376 S.W.2d 336 (Tex. 1964), the Texas Supreme Court held that no wrongful appropriation of trade secrets occurred even though the defendant obtained information regarding plaintiff's patented invention as a result of a license granted to defendant. *Luccous,* 376 S.W.2d at 340. The license was granted during the life of the patent, but was not used or disclosed by defendant license until after the patent expired. *Id.* at 340. The court stated that when the plaintiff filed his patent application, he made an election to secure that protection for his invention for a limited time only "on condition 'that he make full disclosure for the benefit of the public of the manner of making and using the invention.'" *Id.* at 340. The court concluded that the plaintiff's claim of a trade secret was incompatible with the election to surrender the protection of secrecy in return for a patent. *Id.* The court refused to enjoin the defendant from use of the information gained as a result of the license because such information was available to the public, subject only to patent protection. *Id.*

In *Luccous*, the court also distinguished the earlier case of *Hyde Corp. v. Huffines* because the defendant in that case gained his information through a confidential relationship *prior to* the plaintiff's application for a patent. *Id.* at 339. Two years after *Luccous*, the United States Court of Appeals for the Fifth Circuit in *Bryan v. Kershaw*, 366 F.2d 497 (5th Cir. 1966) held that an employee who gains proprietary information in confidence may be enjoined from use of that information even after the device has become public by other means, including a patent. *Bryan*, 366 F.2d at 501-502. Without addressing the decision in *Luccous*, the court concluded that the essence of the tort in Texas is the breach of confidence and not the continuing existence of secrecy. *Id.*

Other decisions in Texas seem to agree with the holding in *Bryan* that the defense of subsequent disclosure through a patent application or through the expiration of a patent is not a valid defense. In *Welex Jet Servs., Inc. v. Owen*, 325 S.W.2d 856 (Tex. Civ. App.—Fort Worth 1959, writ ref'd n.r.e.), the court upheld an injunction, prohibiting two former employees from disclosing information that had been made public through their employer's patent application. *Welex Jet Servs., Inc.*, 325 S.W.2d at 858. Although the timing of that patent application compared to when the employees obtained the confidential information from their employer is not clear, the court expressly rejected the contention that the patent made a public disclosure that destroyed the "secret" nature of the process. *Id.*

In *Thermotics, Inc. v. Bat-Jac Tool Co.*, the court recognized, but distinguished on its facts, the *Luccous* decision, holding that the defendant had appropriated trade secrets consisting of improvements upon and refinements of the product which was the subject of the previously expired patent granted to plaintiff. *Thermotics, Inc.*, 541 S.W.2d 255, 260 (Tex. Civ. App.—Houston [1st Dist.] 1976, no writ). The court repeated the Texas "rule" that the essence of this tort is the breach of a confidential relationship, even though the information may have become public and thus is available for use by everyone except the enjoined defendant. In *Emory Garth ant RTB Tech., Inc. v. Staktek Corp.,* the court affirmed the issuance of a temporary injunction after the date on which the trade secret was publicly disclosed, citing *Hyde* and *K&G.* 876 S.W.2d 545, 548-549 (Tex. App.—Austin 1994, no writ). As the court in *Garth* noted, "Trade secret law is intended to prevent ideas from being directly stolen, rather than copied, and only applies to the small group of people privy to confidential information." *Id.* at 550; see also, *F.S. New Prods. v. Strong Indus.*, 129 S.W.3d 606, 616 (Tex. App. Houston [14th Dist.] 2004, pet. granted).

(b) Limited Disclosure

Although secrecy is required before information can be a trade secret, the secrecy does not have to be absolute. In *Fourtek*, the Fifth Circuit addressed the factors and policies considered to constitute limited disclosure of trade secrets:

> He may without losing his protection
> communicate it to employees involved in
> its use. He may likewise communicate
> it to others pledged to secrecy. Never-
> theless, a substantial element of secrecy
> must exist so that except by the use of
> improper means, there would be difficulty
> in acquiring the information.

Fourtek, 790 F.2d at 1200 (citing Restatement of Torts
§ 757, cmt. b (1939)).

The court concluded that the holder may divulge
his information to a limited extent without destroying
its status as a trade secret. To hold otherwise would
greatly reduce a holder's ability to profit from his
secret. *Id.* "If disclosure to others is made to further
the holder's economic interests, it should in appropriate
circumstances, be considered a limited disclosure that
does not destroy the requisite secrecy." *Id.*

The court cited *Hyde Corp.* and *Sikes* in contending
that subsequent disclosure of a trade secret does not free
one from a constraint of a prior confidential disclosure.
Fourtek, 790 F.2d at 1200. In both of those cases, however, publication of each of the trade secrets by its holder
followed an improper use by one in whom the holder had
confided. The court in *Fourtek* found that the facts before
it could be distinguished from those in *Hyde* and *Sikes*
because (1) the disclosures were not public but only to
businesses with whom the company was dealing; and
(2) the disclosures were made to further the company's
financial interests. *Id.* In *Luccous*, the "trade secret"
has been revealed to all the world through the granting
of a patent on the very information that the party
claimed as its trade secret before any dealing between
the parties.

The employer concerned with protecting the
already-patented product from improper disclosure or use
by an employee should obtain an express non-disclosure
agreement, as well as a non-competition agreement, if
possible. Additionally, refinements or improvements

upon an existing patented product may be entitled to trade secret status if adequately protected from disclosure.

E. The Employment Relationship

Not surprisingly, the tort of misappropriation of trade secrets often involves an employer-employee relationship. In *Hallmark Pers. of Tex. Inc. v. Franks*, 562 S.W.2d 933 (Tex. Civ. App.—Houston [1st Dist.] 1978, no writ), the court announced the general rule that where a defendant breaches a confidential relationship and thereby unfairly uses the trade secret of his or her employer, a cause of action exists to protect the confidential information that the employer maintained as a trade secret.

As noted above, trade secret litigation in the employment context frequently involves "customer lists" and whether those lists are protected trade secrets. In *Mercer v. C. A. Roberts Co.*, 570 F.2d 1232 (5th Cir. 1978), the Fifth Circuit held that a customer list does not necessarily constitute a trade secret under Texas law, even where it contains an analysis of suppliers and the needs and buying habits of customers, if such information is "generally known to any person engaged in this business or can be ascertained by an independent investigation." *Id.* at 1239; see also, *Numed, Inc. v. McNutt*, 724 S.W.2d 432, 435 (Tex. App.—Fort Worth 1987, no writ) (not allowing trade secret protection against employees when information could be learned by independent means); see also *Gary Carpenter & Co. v. Provenzale*, 334 F.3d 450, 468 (5th Cir. 2003); see also *Brooks v. American Biomedical Corp.*, 503 S.W.2d 683

(Tex. Civ. App.—Eastland, 1973, writ ref'd n.r.e.); see also *SCM Corp. v. Triplett Co.*, 399 S.W.2d 583 (Tex. Civ. App.—San Antonio 1966, no writ).

However, other cases have held that information relating to customers, including customer lists, is protected confidential information. The courts therefore enjoined the specific use of the materials and ordered their return. *Miller Paper Co.*, 901 S.W.2d at 601-03; *Collins v. Ryon's Saddle & Ranch Supplies, Inc.*, 576 S.W.2d 914 (Tex. Civ. App.—Fort Worth 1979, no writ); *Expo Chem. Co. v. Brooks*, 572 S.W.2d 8 (Tex. Civ. App.—Houston [1st Dist.] 1978), *rev'd other grounds*, 576 S.W.2d 369 (Tex. 1979) (also recognizing that the factors from the Restatement (Second) of Torts § 757 should be considered when determining whether information given in the employer-employee relationship is a "trade secret").

Counsel representing ex-employees who have left their former employment to begin a competing business may take comfort in the court's recognition that, absent discovery by improper means or breach of confidence, there is nothing *per se* illegal in such actions. In *MPI, Inc. v. Dupre*, 596 S.W.2d 251 (Tex. Civ. App.—Fort Worth 1980, writ ref'd n.r.e.), the court stated:

> The policy of the law is one in approval
> for such to be done. It generally is a
> part of what is called the free enterprise
> system. Now and always such a thing
> is done with the thought of the former
> employees that they will get business
> from those of the customers of the former
> employer with whom they have become

acquainted because of their prior employment upon going into business for themselves. There is nothing legally wrong in
so doing or in making preparation to do
so after contractual termination, though
done prior to the time for that termination. [Citations omitted.] It is only when
an employee uses his official position to
gain a business opportunity that belongs
to his employer or when he actually com-
petes for customers while still employed
that a legal wrong will have accrued.

Id. at 254; see also, *Abetter Trucking Co. v. Arizipe,* 113 S.W.
3d 503, 510 (Tex. App.—Houston [1st Dist.] 2003, no pet.).

F. The Inevitable Disclosure Doctrine

A developing topic in trade secret law as it relates
to employees is the "inevitable disclosure doctrine." As
the name suggests, the theory of inevitable disclosure
is that an employee should not be allowed to compete
with the former employer because he will inevitably
disclose the former employer's trade secrets. In essence,
it allows the employer the benefits of a covenant not to
compete where one did not exist and without satisfying
the statutory requirements. In addition, under this
doctrine, no proof of misappropriation is required, it
is presumed.

The seminal case discussing the inevitable
disclosure doctrine comes from the Seventh Circuit.

See *PepsiCo Inc. v. Redmond,* 54 F.3d 1262 (7th Cir. 1995). Redmond was the general manager for PepsiCo's sports drink business in California. *Id.* at 1264. As such, he was aware of PepsiCo's marketing strategies. When Redmond was hired by one of PepsiCo's direct competitors to work in its sport drink division, PepsiCo sued to prevent Redmond from working for the competitor. *Id.* at 1265-66. Although Redmond was not subject to a non-compete agreement, the court prevented him from working for the competitor for six months based on inevitable disclosure. *Id.* Under that doctrine, a court should enjoin an employee's employment with a new employer if:

(1) the former employer and the new employer are competitors;

(2) the employee's new position is comparable to his or her former position; and

(3) the new employee will inevitably disclose the former employer's trade secrets irrespective of his good faith attempt not to.

Id. at 1270. Although to date, no reported Texas case has expressly adopted the inevitable disclosure doctrine, *Elec. Data Sys., Corp. v. Powell*, 524 S.W.2d 393 (Tex. Civ. App. –Dallas 1975, writ ref'd n.r.e.) and *Weed Eater, Inc. v. Dowling*, 562 S.W.2d 898 (Tex. Civ. App.—Houston [1st Dist.] 1978, writ ref'd n.r.e.) are often cited for the proposition that Texas recognizes the inevitable disclosure doctrine. But both cases address the enforceability of a covenant not to compete and neither uses the term "inevitable disclosure." See *Electronic Data Sys., Corp.*, 524 S.W.2d at 398; see also *Weed Eater,*

Inc., 562 S.W.2d at 902. Furthermore, both cases were decided before the enactment of §§ 15.50-15.52 of the Texas Business and Commerce Code that now govern covenants not to compete.

Texas courts have granted injunctions where the use or disclosure of confidential information was *probable.* See *T-N-T Motorsports*, 965 S.W.2d at 24; see also *Rugen*, 864 S.W.2d at 552; see also *Conley v. DSC Communications Corp.*, No. 05-98-01051-CV, 1999 WL 89955 (Tex. App.—Dallas Feb. 24, 1999, no pet.). Those seeking relief in Texas should therefore frame the theory as one of probable disclosure instead of or in addition to inevitable disclosure.

In determining whether an injunction should issue in a "probable disclosure" case, the Dallas Court of Appeals considered the following factors important: misconduct on the part of the departing employee; the new employer's need for the information; and the similarity between the employee's former and current positions. *Conley*, 1999 WL at *5-7. Other courts have considered additional factors. See, e.g., *La Calhene, Inc. v. Spolyar*, 938 F. Supp. 523, 530 (W.D. Wis. 1996) (considering whether the industry is highly competitive); see also *Ram Prods. Co. v. Chaincey,* 967 F. Supp. 1071, 1087 (N.D. Ind. 1997) (considering whether actual disclosure has occurred); see also *Lumex, Inc. v. Highsmith*, 919 F. Supp. 624, 633 (E.D.N.Y. 1996) (considering the credibility of the defendants); see also *PepsiCo Inc.*, 54 F.3d at 1271 (considering the new employer's efforts to protect the former employer's trade secrets).

G. Injunctive Relief

The primary relief sought in Texas for theft of trade secrets is an injunction. See *Weed Eater, Inc.,* 562 S.W.2d at 898. Injunctive relief is appropriate to prevent the disclosure of confidential information that the employer maintained as a trade secret. See *Picker Int'l, Inc. v. Blanton,* 756 F. Supp. at 980; see also *Zoecon Indus.,* 713 F.2d at 1179. Injunctive relief is especially appropriate where an employee seeks to disclose or use confidential information acquired through specialized training provided by the former employer. *Picker,* 756 F. Supp. at 980. Injunctive relief has, on occasion, extended to enjoining a third-party assignee who received trade secrets from a former employee. In *Bryan v. Kershaw,* 366 F.2d 497 (5th Cir. 1966), the court approved the granting of injunctive relief against a third party to whom the former employee-defendant had assigned the confidential information, thereby refusing to allow the third party "to reap the benefits of the illegally gained competitive advantage." *Id.* at 503.

H. Damages

(1) Actual Damages

Recovery of actual damages may also be appropriate. The United States Court of Appeals for the Fifth Circuit has held that damages in the form of plaintiff's losses *and* defendant's profits are appropriate in a breach of contract case relating to trade secret matters. *Sikes v. McGraw-Edison Co.*, 665 F.2d 731, 737 (5th Cir. 1982). In *Sikes*, the Fifth Circuit upheld a $900,000 award of damages for a breach of contract based on a letter agreement that was, in essence, a nondisclosure agreement. In reaching its decision, the court relied on *Univ. Computing Co. v. Lykes-Youngstown Corp.*, 504 F.2d 518, 535-37 (5th Cir. 1974) (en banc).

In that case, the Fifth Circuit gave an exhaustive discussion of damages in the trade secret arena. In pertinent part, the court stated:

> The law governing protection of trade secrets essentially is designed to regulate unfair business competition, and is not a substitute for criminal laws against theft or other civil remedies for conversion. If the defendant enjoyed actual profits, a type of restitutionary remedy can be afforded the plaintiff—either recovering the full total of defendant's profits or some apportioned amount designed to correspond to the actual contribution the plaintiff's trade secret made to the defendant's commercial success. Because the primary concern in most cases is to measure the value to the defendant of what he actually obtained from the plaintiff, the proper measure is to calculate what the parties would have agreed to as a fair price for licensing the defendant to put the trade secret to the use the defendant intended at the time the misappropriation took place.

While *Light* spells out the factors that must be met, application of the factors by the courts has proven to be difficult and inconsistent.

A typical example of a covenant ancillary to an otherwise enforceable agreement arises when an employer gives an employee confidential and proprietary information or trade secrets in exchange for the employee's promise not to disclose them.[2]

Importantly, for disclosure of trade secrets to serve as consideration sufficient to support a covenant not to compete, the disclosure must be after the parties enter into the covenant. Otherwise, it is past consideration, which cannot be sufficient consideration. See *Bandit Messenger of Austin v. Contreras*, 2000 U.S. LEXIS 7166 (Tex. App.—Austin 2000, no pet.).

The court in *Light* pointed out that the same standard applies to employees at-will as to employees with written contracts for a certain term. An at-will employee can have an "otherwise enforceable agreement" with the employer as long as the consideration for a promise

---

[2]   *Id*. at 647 n.14. The court reasoned that such an agreement is enforceable because (1) the consideration given by the employer [the trade secrets] in the otherwise enforceable agreement [exchange of trade secrets for promise not to disclose them] gives rise to the employer's interest in restraining the employee from competing [employee would have knowledge of employer's trade secrets]; and (2) the covenant is designed to enforce the employee's consideration [the promise not to disclose the trade secrets] in the otherwise enforceable agreement. See *id.* Importantly, it is the obligation to provide the trade secret and not a statement that they may be provided that serves as the consideration by the employer. Additionally, because this agreement is independent from the employment agreement, it is an "otherwise enforceable agreement" under the statute.

is not dependend on a period of employment. Such a promise, the court noted "would be illusory because it fails to bind the promisor who always retains the option of discontinuing employment in lieu of performance." *Id.* at 646.

Despite the decision in *Light*, drafting an enforceable covenant not to compete can be difficult, and courts often have difficulty applying *Light* and the statute. Accordingly, it is an area ripe for litigation. If you represent the employee, you are likely to challenge the covenant not to compete as failing to meet the requirements of the statute and the *Light* decision. Conversely, if you represent the employer, you will need to establish that the covenant satisfies the requirements of the statue and *Light*. Even if the agreement is found to be unenforceable, you will possibly have other causes of action to pursue.

The second statutory requirement for a covenant not to compete to be enforceable is that it contain limitations as to time, geographic area, and scope of activity that are reasonable. Tex. Bus. & Com. Code Ann. § 15.50(a) (Vernon Supp. 2005). The question of what is reasonable is a question of law for the court. See *CRC-Evans Pipeline Intern. v. Myers*, 927 S.W.2d 259, 263 (Tex. App.—Houston [1st Dist.] 1996, no writ). Accordingly, there are no firm standards regarding time, geographic area or scope of activity. Some general guidelines, however, have been established.

As for the duration of a covenant not to compete, the nature of the industry will have a significant impact on the enforceability of the term. In a highly technical and quickly changing industry, a six-month term may be reasonable. Other courts have found two-year post-employment restrictions reasonable. See, e.g., *Osborn v. Bell Helicopter Textron, Inc.*, 828 F. Supp. 446, 450 (N.D. Tex. 1993); see also *Prop. Tax Assocs., Inc. v. Staffeldt*, 800 S.W.2d 349, 350 (Tex. App.—El Paso 1990, writ denied).What constitutes a reasonable geographic restriction is generally the territory in which the employee worked while employed. See *Zep Mfg. Co. v. Harthcock*, 824 S.W.2d 654, 660 (Tex. App.—Dallas 1992, no writ). The scope of activity restricted should be limited to the activity the employee performed while employed. Additionally, if the occupation involved personal services, the restraint should be limited to the clients or customers with whom the employee dealt during his employment. See *John R. Ray & Sons, Inc. v. Stroman*, 923 S.W.2d 80, 85 (Tex. App.—Houston [14th Dist.] 1996, no writ).

While both requirements for enforceability must be met and both are questions of law, the statute provides an important difference between the two. If the covenant not to compete is not ancillary to an otherwise enforceable agreement, then the covenant is not enforceable. However, if the covenant meets the first requirement but the court finds its limitations unreasonable, the court will reform the covenant to make it reasonable. The court's willingness to reform the covenant is commonly described as the "blue pencil rule." Some states, for example Arkansas, do not have such a blue-pencil rule. Thus, if the non-compete agreement contains an overly broad provision in a "non-blue pencil" state, the court will not reform the agreement and it will be deemed unenforceable.

The Texas statute allowing reformation of the agreement states:

> If the covenant is found to be ancillary to or part of an otherwise enforceable agreement but contains limitations as to time, geographical area, or scope of activity to be restrained that are not reasonable and impose a greater restraint than is necessary to protect the goodwill or other business interest of the promisee, the court *shall* reform the covenant to the extent necessary . . . and enforce the covenant as reformed . . .

Tex. Bus. & Com. Code Ann. § 15.51(c) (Vernon Supp. 2005).

Accordingly, if the covenant is otherwise enforceable, the trial court has a duty to reform the covenant to provide reasonable limitations. See *Zep Mfg. Co.*, 824 S.W.2d at 661. If the trial court denies an injunction seeking to enforce a covenant not to compete, the company or individual seeking the injunction can immediately appeal the order. Tex. Civ. Prac. & Rem. Code Ann. § 51.014 (Vernon Supp. 2005). The appellate court can only consider the denial of the injunction. It cannot consider whether the trial court should have reformed the covenant. See *McNeilus Companies, Inc. v. Sams*, 971 S.W.2d 507 (Tex. App.—Dallas 1997, no writ). If the court reforms the covenant, the plaintiff is limited to injunctive relief. Tex. Bus. & Com. Code Ann. § 15.51(c) (Vernon Supp. 2005).

business. See e.g., *Advanced Ross Elec.*, 624 S.W.2d at 318 (the duty obligates the employee to act for the sole benefit of her employer and to do nothing to injure the employer's financial or business interests). This implied duty includes a duty not to use trade secrets in a manner adverse to the employer and it prevents a former employee from using confidential information or trade secrets acquired during the course of employment. See *Am. Derringer Corp. v. Bond*, 924 S.W.2d 773, 777 (Tex. App.—Waco 1996, no writ); *T-N-T Motorsports*, 965 S.W.2d at 21-22.

Accordingly, even though the employee has not signed an employment, confidentiality and/or non-disclosure agreement, common law prevents the use of a former employer's trade secrets and confidential information. See *Miller Paper*, 901 S.W.2d at 603.

This duty, however, does not prevent a former employee from using any general knowledge, skills, and experience acquired during his employment to compete with his former employer. See *Picker Int'l, Inc. v. Blanton*, 756 F. Supp. 971, 979 (N.D. Tex. 1990). Rather, what is to be protected must concern specific, secret information such as customer lists, pricing information, client information, customer preferences, buyer contacts, market strategies, blueprints, drawings, or a mechanical device or process. *Id.*; see also *T-N-T Motorsports, Inc.*, 965 S.W.2d at 22.

(4) Computer Fraud and Abuse Act

A relatively new development in trade secret litigation is the use of the Computer Fraud and Abuse

Act ("CFAA"). 18 U.S.C. § 1030. The CFAA is a criminal statute that provides, in part, that "whoever . . . intentionally accesses a computer without authorization or exceeds authorized access, and thereby obtains . . . information from any protected computer if the conduct involved an interstate or foreign communication . . . shall be punished." *Id.* § 1030(a)(2)(C). As the language indicates, one important feature of the CFAA, is that it protects any information stored on a computer, whether or not that that information is a secret.

The CFAA, however, also provides for a civil cause of action. It states that "any person who suffers damage or loss by reason of a violation of this section may maintain a civil action against the violator to obtain compensatory damages and injunctive relief or other equitable relief." *Id.* § 1030(g). Although there are very few reported cases on the CFAA, it is another possible cause of action that should be considered, especially if the plaintiff desires access to the federal courts.[3]

(5) Criminal Liability

Finally, misappropriation of trade secrets could lead to criminal liability. The Texas Penal Code makes the theft of trade secrets a third degree felony and defines a trade secret as "the whole or any part of any scientific

---

[3] For example, a plaintiff might determine that the local state courts were historically unwilling to find the type of information plaintiff sought to protect a "trade secret." Not only might the federal district court be more willing to protect the information, the CFAA addresses the protection of information on a protected computer, rather than trade secrets. See 18 U.S.C. §1030(a)(2)(C). Accordingly, it is unclear whether a plaintiff would even be required to prove that "trade secrets" were involved.

or technical information, design, process, procedure, formula, or improvement that has value and that the owners has taken measure to prevent from becoming available to persons other than those selected by the owner to have access for limited purposes." Tex. Pen. Code § 31.05 (Vernon 2005).

In addition to the CFAA, theft of trade secrets is potentially a federal criminal offense under the Economic Espionage Act ("EEA"). Although the statute was passed in response to concerns about the flow of trade secret information to foreign entities it also criminalizes *any* theft of trade secrets. 18 U.S.C. §§ 1831, 1832.

With respect to the theft of trade secrets, the EEA provides:

(a) Whoever, with intent to convert a trade secret, that is related to or included in a product that is produced for or placed in interstate or foreign commerce, to the economic benefit of anyone other than the owner thereof, and intending or knowing that the offense will injure any owner of that trade secret, knowingly

  (1) steals, or without authorization appropriates, takes, carries away, or conceals, or by fraud, artifice, or deception obtains such information;

  (2) without authorization copies, duplicates, sketches, draws, photographs, downloads, uploads, alters, destroys, photocopies, repli-

cates, transmits, delivers, sends, mails, communicates, or conveys such information;

(3) receives, buys, or possesses such information, knowing the same to have been stolen or appropriated, obtained, or converted without authorization;

(4) attempts to commit any offense described in paragraphs (1) through (3); or

(5) conspires with one or more other persons to commit any offense described in paragraphs (1) through (3), and one or more of such persons do any act to effect the object of the conspiracy,

shall, except as provided in subsection (b), be fined under this title or imprisoned not more than 10 years, or both.

(b) Any organization that commits any offense described in subsection (a) shall be fined not more than $5,000,000.

18 U.S.C. § 1832.

The EEA is relatively new and few cases have been reported addressing its application.[4] As can be seen from

---

[4] But a recent example of an EEA prosecution involves a former employee for Cisco. The FBI confiscated three CDROMs at the defendant's apartment containing information from Cisco. The former Cisco manager allegedly confessed that he had downloaded software from Cisco to use as a reference tool at his new job. Although he gave Cisco notice of his resignation in September 2000, he continued to log on from home through October. Additionally, he entered the Cisco premises and logged on to a terminal of a co-worker on vacation and burned several CD ROMs. See *U.S. v. Morch*, No. 3-00-3052 (N.D. Calif. 2000).

the plain language of the statute, severe penalties, in both jail time and fines can be imposed.

Only the federal government can bring an action under the EEA. Both plaintiffs and defendants in civil litigation, however, should keep in mind that the EEA, CFAA and the Texas Penal Code provide the possibility of criminal liability in addition to civil liability.

VII. NEGLIGENT MISREPRESENTATION

A. Introduction
B. Definition and Elements
   (1) Persons Liable
   (2) Statements that Give Rise to a Cause of Action
C. Damages
D. Examples

A. Introduction

Texas courts recognize negligent misrepresentation as a separate and independent cause of action. In defining the tort, Texas courts have adopted the specific terms of Section 552 of the Restatement (Second) of Torts ("Section 552"). Texas first adopted Section 552 in *Federal Bank Ass'n of Tyler v. Sloane,* 825 S.W.2d 439, 442 (Tex. 1991). Section 552 provides:

> (1) One who, in the course of his business, profession, or employment, or in any other transaction in which he has a pecuniary interest, supplies false information for the guidance of others in their

business transactions, is subject to liability for pecuniary loss caused to them by their justifiable reliance upon the information, if he fails to exercise reasonable care or competence in obtaining or communicating the information;

(2) Except as stated in Subsection (3), the liability stated in Subsection (1) is limited to loss suffered (a) by the person or one of a limited group of persons for whose benefit and guidance he intends to supply the information or knows that the recipient intends to supply it; and (b) through reliance upon it in a transaction that he intends the information to influence or knows that the recipient so intends or in a substantially similar transaction; and

(3) The liability of one who is under a public duty to give the information extends to loss suffered by any of the class of persons for whose benefit the duty is created, in any of the transactions in which it is intended to protect them.

Restatement (Second) of Torts § 552 (1977).

A negligent misrepresentation cause of action has a two-year statute of limitations and must be filed no later than two years after the day the cause of action accrues. *Texas Am. Corp. v. Woodbridge Joint Venture*, 809 S.W.2d 299, 302-03 (Tex. App.—Fort Worth 1991, writ denied). In Texas, the discovery rule exception applies to negligent misrepresentation causes of action and may extend the deadline by which a suit must be filed. *Sabine Towing & Transp. Co., Inc. v. Holliday Ins. Agency, Inc.,* 54 S.W.3d 57, 60-61 (Tex. App.—Texarkana 2001, pet. denied). The discovery rule defers the accrual of a cause of action until the plaintiff knew, or through the exercise of reasonable diligence should have known, of the facts giving rise to the cause of action. *Id.* The discovery rule apples to a claim for negligent misrepresentation if: (1) the injury is inherently undiscoverable and (2) the evidence of the injury is objectively verifiable. *Velsicol Chem. Corp. v. Winograd*, 956 S.W.2d 529, 531 (Tex. 1997).

B. Definition and Elements

Expressly agreeing with section 552, the Texas Supreme Court in *Sloane* set forth its own elements of the negligent misrepresentation cause of action:

(1) the representation is made by a defendant in the course of his business, or in a transaction in which he has a pecuniary interest;

(2) the defendant supplies "false information" for the guidance of others in their business;

(3) the defendant did not exercise reasonable care or competence in obtaining or communicating the information; and

(4) the plaintiff suffers a pecuniary loss by justifiably relying on the representation.

825 S.W.2d at 442; *First Nat'l Bank of Durant v. Trans Terra Corp. Int'l*, 142 F.3d 802, 809 (5th Cir. 1998). Unlike common-law fraud, negligent misrepresentation does not require knowledge of the falsity or reckless disregard of the truth or falsity of the representation at the time it was made. *Larsen v. Carlene Langford & Assocs., Inc.*, 41 S.W.3d 245, 250 (Tex. App.—Waco 2001, pet. denied).

(1) Persons Liable

Liability is extended to persons or a class of persons whom the maker of the representation intends to benefit or who foreseeably may be expected to act in reliance on the representation. *Hermann Hosp. v. Nat'l Standard Ins. Co.*, 776 S.W.2d 249, 254 (Tex. App.—Houston [1st Dist.] 1989, writ denied). Section 552 requires actual knowledge of the recipient's identity and a specific intent on the part of the alleged tortfeasor that the claimant would rely on the misrepresentation. *Trans-Gulf Corp. v. Performance Aircraft Serv., Inc,* 82 S.W.3d 691, 696 (Tex. App.—Eastland 2002, no pet.) (holding repair shop was not liable for entries into maintenance record log books for aircraft purchased by future owners because no evidence that repair shop knew future owners when the repair work was performed or that maintenance record would be supplied to this future owner).

Texas courts have used Section 552 to hold other processionals liable to third parties. Specifically, Texas courts have recognized a cause of action for negligent misrepresentation against auditors, real estate brokers, securities placement agents, accountants, surveyors, title insurers, attorneys, physicians and insurance agents. *Nast v. State Farm Fire and Cas. Co.*, 82 S.W.3d 114, 124 (Tex. App.—San Antonio 2002, no pet.).

(2) Statements that Give Rise to a Cause of Action

The misrepresentation must be of existing fact, not a breach of a future promise. *Young Ref. Corp. v. Pennzoil Co.*, 46 S.W.3d 380, 388-389 (Tex. App.—Houston [1st

Dist.] 2001, no pet.). Furthermore, the representation must be of false information, not merely misleading information. *Continental Sav. Ass'n v. Collins*, 814 S.W.2d 829, 833 (Tex. App.—Houston [14th Dist.] 1991, no writ).

C. Damages

A plaintiff is not entitled to recover for negligent misrepresentation unless the plaintiff was actually damaged by the misrepresentation. *Bellatti v. Holland Mort. and Inv. Corp.*, 838 S.W.2d 261-263 (Tex. App.— Texarkana 1992, no writ) (without proof that she could have obtained financing from some other source, loan applicant failed to show that she was damaged by mortgage company's negligence). In negligent misrepresentation cases with contract claims, the Texas Supreme Court requires that the plaintiff prove tort injury independent of contract damages. *D.S.A., Inc. v. Hillsboro Indep. Sch. Dist.*, 973 S.W.2d 662-664 (Tex. 1998). The independent injury element is required in negligent misrepresentation cases because elimination of this element would "potentially convert every contract interpretation dispute into a negligent misrepresentation claim." *Id.* at 664.

Texas adopts the measurement of damages as set forth in the Section 552B. See *Sloane*, 825 S.W.2d at 442. Section 552B states, in relevant part:

(1) the damages recoverable for a negligent misrepresentation are those necessary to compensate the

> plaintiff for the pecuniary loss to him of which the misrepresentation is legal cause, including:
> (a) the difference between the value of what he has received in the transaction and its pu chase price or other value given for it; and
> (b) pecuniary loss suffered otherwise as a co sequence of the plaintiff's reliance upon the misrepresentation.
> (2) the damages recoverable for a negligent misrepresentation do not include the benefit of the plaintiff's contract with the defendant.

Restatement (Second) of Torts § 552B (1977). Damages for negligent misrepresentation are limited to pecuniary losses. *D.S.A., Inc.,* 973 S.W.2d at 663-664. Section 552(B) excludes benefit-of-the-bargain damages as an available measure of damages. *Sloane,* 825 S.W.2d at 443. Therefore, a plaintiff may not recover lost profits related to a transaction. *Id.*; but see *Texas Commerce Bank Reagan v. Lebco Constructors, Inc.,* 865 S.W.2d 68, 75-76 (Tex. App.—Corpus Christi 1993, writ denied) (Permitting lost profits to the extent the profits expected under a contract are recoverable as consequential damages). Mental anguish damages are not a type of pecuniary loss and therefore are not available in a negligent misrepresentation case. *Sloane,* 825 S.W.2d at 442-43.

D. Examples

(1) Absence of an attorney-client relationship does not prevent a third party from suing an attorney for negligent misrepresentation under Section 552. *McCamish, Martin,*

Brown & Loeffler v. F.E. Appling Interests, 991 S.W.2d 787, 791 (Tex. 1999).

(2) Under Section 552, a surveyor could be held liable to a landowner not in privity with the surveyor for negligent misrepresentation. *Cook Consultants, Inc. v. Larson,* 700 S.W.2d 231, 234-35 (Tex. App.—Dallas 1985, writ ref'd n.r.e.).

(3) An accountant preparing audited financial statements will not be liable for injuries to persons relying on the statements without actual knowledge of reliance. See *Abrams Centre Natl. Bank v. Farmer, Fuq ua & Huff, P.C.,* 2005 W.L. 2806316 (Tex. App.—El Paso 2005); *cf. Blue Bell, Inc. v. Peat, Marwick, Mitchell & Co.,* 715 S.W.2d 408 (Tex. App.—Dallas 1986, writ ref'd n.r.e.).

VIII. Tortious Interference with Contractual and Business Relations

A. Introduction

The related torts of tortious interference with contracts and tortious interference with business relations are recognized in virtually all states, including Texas. W. Prosser & W. Keeton, The Law of Torts, § 129, 980 (5th ed. 1984); see *Piper v. Chris-Craft Indus., Inc.*, 430 U.S. 1, 40-41 (1977) (recognizing "common-law principles of interference with a prospective commercial advantage"). Such interference claims originated in the master-servant context, but over time have been extended to all types of business relationships. However, recent opinions by the Texas Supreme Court may mark a trend toward reining in the growing scope of the tortious interference theory, at least with respect to claims for interference with prospective business relations.

B. Tortious Interference with Existing Contracts

The tort of tortious interference with existing contracts was first recognized by the Texas Supreme Court in the employment context. *Raymond v. Yarrington*,

73 S.W. 800 (Tex. 1903). Since then, Texas courts have expanded the doctrine to apply to any contract. *State Nat'l Bank v. Farah Mfg. Co.*, 678 S.W.2d 661, 689 (Tex. App.—El Paso 1984, writ dism'd by agr.); *Hughes v. Houston Northwest Med. Ctr.*, 680 S.W.2d 838, 842 (Tex. App.—Houston [1st Dist.] 1984, writ ref'd n.r.e.), *cert. denied*, 106 S.Ct. 571 (1985).

(1) Definition and Elements

Interference has been defined as "all intentional invasions of contractual relations, including any act injuring or destroying property and so interfering with the performance of the contract itself, regardless of whether breach of contract is induced." *Farah*, 678 S.W.2d at 689. The elements of tortious interference with an existing contract include: (1) the plaintiff had a valid contract with a third party; (2) the defendant willfully and intentionally interfered with the contract; (3) such interference was the proximate cause of the plaintiff's injury; and (4) the plaintiff incurred actual damage or loss. *Prudential Ins. Co. v. Fin. Review Servs., Inc.*, 29 S.W.3d 74, 77-78 (Tex. 2000); *Victoria Bank & Trust Co. v. Brady*, 811 S.W.2d 931, 939 (Tex. 1991); *Juliette Fowler Homes, Inc. v. Welch Assoc., Inc.*, 793 S.W.2d 660, 664 (Tex. 1990).

(a) Contract in Existence

To prevail on a cause of action for tortious interference with a contract, there must be a *valid* and existing contract subject to interference. *Juliette Fowler Homes, Inc.*, 793 S.W.2d at 664; *Steinmetz & Assoc., Inc. v. Crow*, 700 S.W.2d 276, 277 n. 1 (Tex. App.—San Antonio 1985, writ ref'd n.r.e.). Where a contract has terminated, there is no contractual relationship with which to interfere. *Ice Bros., Inc. v. Bannowsky*, 840 S.W.2d 57, 63 (Tex. App.—El Paso 1992, no writ).

If the contract is *void* as illegal or against public policy, its unenforceability is a complete defense to the tortious interference claim. *Travel Masters, Inc. v. Star Tours, Inc.*, 827 S.W.2d 830, 833 (Tex. 1991) (noting that an unenforceable covenant not to compete will not form the basis of a tortious interference action); *Ralston Purina Co. v. McKendrick*, 850 S.W.2d 629, 638-39 (Tex. App.—San Antonio 1993, writ denied) (stating that "a contract to do a thing which cannot be performed without a violation of law is void"); *Juliette Fowler Homes, Inc.*, 793 S.W.2d at 664-65; see also *NCH Corp. v. Share Corp.*, 757 F.2d 1540, 1543 (5th Cir. 1985) (citing Restatement (Second) of Torts § 774 (1977)) (finding no liability for interfering with an illegal agreement or an agreement effecting a violation of public policy). A contract is illegal if (1) the contract or its performance violates a constitution, statute or ordinance; (2) the contract is contrary to public policy; or (3) the contract is an agreement to use the subject matter thereof for an unlawful purpose. *GNG Gas Sys., Inc. v. Dean*, 921 S.W.2d 421, 427 (Tex. App.—Amarillo 1996, writ denied). Additionally, a contract made with a view of violating the laws of another country, "though not obnoxious to either the forum or of the place where the contract is made," is illegal. *McKendrick*, 850 S.W.2d at 639.

However, if the contract is merely *voidable* and not against public policy, such as where the statute of frauds might apply to bar the agreement, then unenforceability of the contract is no defense to a tortious interference claim. *Hi-Line Elec. Co. v. Dowco Elec. Prod.*, 765 F.2d 1359, 1362 (5th Cir. 1985) (discussing *Clements v. Withers*, 437 S.W.2d 818 (Tex. 1969)).

(b) Contract With Non-Defendant Third Party

A party cannot willfully and intentionally interfere with his own contract. *Holloway v. Skinner*, 898 S.W.2d 793, 795 (Tex. 1995); *WesTex Abilene Assocs., L.P. v. Franco*, 3 S.W.3d 45, 49 (Tex. App.—Eastland 1999, no pet.) (holding that liability for tortious interference with an existing contract must be premised on the acts of a stranger to the contract); *Hoggett v. Brown,* 971 S.W.2d 472, 493 (Tex. App.—Houston [14th Dist.] 1997, pet. denied) (noting that the person who induces the breach cannot be a contracting party). Although this rule seems simple enough, it is sometimes difficult to apply to a corporation, which acts only through its agents.

A corporate agent cannot be liable for interference with the corporation's contract unless the agent acted intentionally and willfully to serve his own personal interests at the expense of his corporate principal's interests. *Powell Indus., Inc. v. Allen*, 985 S.W.2d 455, 457 (Tex. 1998); see also *Latch v. Gratty, Inc.,* 107 S.W.3d 543, 545 (Tex. 2003) (*per curium*). Whether an agent willfully and intentionally interferes with a principal's contracts to serve his own interests is a fact issue for a jury to determine. *Abetter Trucking Co. v. Arizpe,* 113 S.W.3d 503, 509 (Tex. App.—Houston [1st Dist.] 2003, no pet.). The mere existence of a personal stake in the outcome cannot alone constitute proof the agent committed an act of willful or intentional interference. *Ed Rachal Found. v. D'Unger,* 117 S.W.3d 348, 366 (Tex. App.—Corpus Christi

2003, pet. filed). Thus, if the evidence shows that the agent acted to benefit himself, as well as his corporate principal, then the evidence is insufficient to establish liability against the agent. *Powell Indus.*, 985 S.W.2d at 457 (noting that proof of mixed motives to benefit himself and his principal are insufficient).

Texas appellate courts are split on the question of whether a parent and subsidiary are considered one entity for purposes of a tortious interference analysis. The United States Fifth Circuit Court of Appeals was the first court to hold that under Texas law a parent corporation could not interfere with a subsidiary's contracts. See *Deauville Corp. v. Federated Dept. Stores, Inc.*, 756 F.2d 1183, 1196-97 (5th Cir. 1985). In 1987, the Houston First Court of Appeals followed the Fifth Circuit in *Deauville* and held that a parent and its wholly-owned subsidiary's interests are so closely aligned that it is impossible as a matter of law for one to tortiously interfere with the other's contracts. See *Baker v. Welch*, 735 S.W.2d 548, 550 (Tex. App.—Houston [1st Dist.] 1987, writ dism'd). The majority of Texas appellate courts confronting the issue have followed *Deauville* and *Baker* and have held that parents and their wholly-owned subsidiaries are incapable of interfering with each other's contracts. See *Schoellkopf v. Pledger*, 778 S.W.2d 897, 903-04 (Tex. App.—Dallas 1989, writ denied); *American Med. Int'l, Inc. v. Giurintano*, 821 S.W.2d 331, 336-37 (Tex. App.—Houston [14th Dist.] 1991, no writ); *Grizzle v. Texas Commerce Bank, N.A.*, 38 S.W.3d 265, 286-87 (Tex. App.—Dallas 2001), *rev'd on other grounds*, 96 S.W.3d 240 (Tex. 2002).

However, in 1997, the San Antonio Court of Appeals broke from the majority of Texas appellate courts holding

of exclusive distribution system was sufficient to show defendant knew of the existence of contracts); but see *Frost Nat'l Bank v. Alamo Nat'l Bank*, 421 S.W.2d 153, 156 (Tex. App.—San Antonio 1967, writ ref'd n.r.e.) (proof of actual knowledge of contract required; proof of notice insufficient). A plaintiff must show more than mere suspicion of a contract. *Steinmetz & Assocs., Inc. v. Crow*, 700 S.W.2d 276, 277-78 (Tex. App.—San Antonio 1985, writ ref'd n.r.e.). Mere knowledge of a party's contractual obligations to someone else will not give rise to tort liability without the defendant's act of interference—i.e., persuading a party to breach by offering better terms or other incentives. *Davis v. HydPro, Inc.*, 839 S.W.2d 137, 139 (Tex. App.—Eastland 1992, writ denied); see also *John Paul Mitchell*, 17 S.W.3d at 731-32 (finding no willful or intentional interference, where there was no evidence that defendant persuaded anyone to breach its contractual obligations to the plaintiff).

(d) Proximate Cause of Damage

To hold a defendant liable for interfering with a contract, there must be evidence that the defendant actually caused or brought about injury to the performance of the contract. *Hill v. Heritage Res., Inc.*, 964 S.W.2d 89, 126 (Tex. App.—El Paso 1997, pet. denied); *Scott v. Galusha*, 890 S.W.2d 945, 951 (Tex. App.—Fort Worth 1994, writ denied) (finding no tortious interference where there was no harm to plaintiff's business). Taking an active part in persuading a party to breach a contract is part of the proximate cause requirement. *Davis*, 839 S.W.2d at 139-40.

(e) Damages or Loss

Tortious interference requires that the plaintiff suffer actual damage or loss as a result of the tortious interference with the contract. *Anderson, Greenwood & Co. v. Martin*, 44 S.W.3d 200, 219 (Tex. App.—Houston [14th Dist.] 2001, pet. denied). Damages must be established with reasonable certainty, but the amount need not be absolutely certain. *Browning-Ferris, Inc. v. Reyna*, 852 S.W.2d 540, 548 (Tex .App.—San Antonio,1992), *rev'd on other grounds*, 865 S.W.2d 925 (Tex. 1993); see also *Reyna v. First Nat'l Bank in Edinburg,* 55 S.W.3d 58, 70 (Tex. App.—Corpus Christi 2001, no pet.) (plaintiff's testimony that he could not do business with the vendors after his termination based upon "speculation based on my common sense" was insufficient evidence of damages necessary to recover on a tortious interference claim).

The measure of actual damages for tortious interference with a contract is the same as the measure of damages for breach of contract—namely, attempting to put the plaintiff in the same economic position he would have been in if the contract interfered with had been fully performed. *Am. Nat'l Petro. Co. v. Transcon. Gas Pipe Line Corp.*, 798 S.W.2d 274, 278 (Tex. 1990); see also *Anderson, Greenwood & Co. v. Martin,* 44 S.W.3d 200, 219 (Tex. App.—Houston [14th Dist.] 2001, pet. denied); *Capital Title Co., Inc. v. Donaldson*, 739 S.W.2d 384, 391 (Tex. App.—Houston [1st Dist.] 1987, no writ). In some instances, however, basic contract damages are insufficient and the entire range of tort damages may be recoverable. *Exxon Corp. v. Allsup,* 808 S.W.2d 648, 660-61 (Tex. App.—Corpus Christi 1991, writ denied). In such instances, a successful plaintiff in a tortious interference with contract case may be entitled to recover: (1) the pecuniary loss of the benefit of the contract or prospective relation; (2) consequential losses for which the interference is the legal cause; and (3) emotional distress of actual harm to reputation, if they are reasonably considered to result from the interference. *Id.* at 660 (citing Restatement (Second) of Torts § 774A (1977)). Also, a plaintiff may recover for injury to reputation and lost profits. *Browning-Ferris*, 852 S.W.2d at 548-49.

Additionally, a plaintiff may recover under an unjust enrichment theory where the plaintiff's lost profits are not readily ascertainable. *Sandare Chem. Co. v. WAKO Int'l, Inc.*, 820 S.W.2d 21, 23-24 (Tex. App.—Fort Worth 1991, no writ) (plaintiff may recover defendant's profits if plaintiff is unable to show with certainty the profits it would have realized).

(2) Exemplary Damages

Exemplary damages are available in an action for tortious interference with a contract where the tortfeasor acted with actual malice. *Exxon Corp.*, 808 S.W.2d at 661. Actual malice is defined at common law as ill-will, spite, evil motive, or purposing the injuring of another. *Corporate Wings, Inc. v. King,* 767 S.W.2d 485, 487 (Tex. App.—Dallas 1989, no writ). Applying this definition, courts would traditionally imply malice when the defendant's interfering conduct was found to be intentional. *Cont'l Coffee Prods. Co. v. Cazarez*, 937 S.W.2d 444, 452 (Tex. 1996) ("Implied or legal malice . . . exists when wrongful conduct is intentional and without just cause or excuse").

Chapter 41 of the Texas Civil Practice and Remedies Code modifies the common-law definition of actual malice and the standards necessary to show such malice. To recover exemplary damages under Chapter 41, the plaintiff must prove by clear and convincing evidence that the defendant acted with actual malice. Previous versions of Chapter 41 defined malice as either the specific intent to cause substantial injury or conscious indifference. The new version of Chapter 41, effective September 1, 2003, limits the definition of malice to include only the "specific intent by the defendant to cause substantial injury or harm to the claimant." Tex. Civ. Prac. & Rem. Code Ann. §§ 41.003(a), 41.006 (Vernon 2004). Thus, it now appears that a plaintiff must prove that the defendant specifically intended to cause the resulting harm; whereas, under common law, the plaintiff arguably only had to prove that the interfering conduct was intentional. Further, to recover exemplary damages under the new version of Chapter 41, the plaintiff must obtain a unanimous jury finding as to the tortious interference claim, the malice finding, and the amount of exemplary damages. Tex. Civ. Prac. & Rem. Code Ann. § 41.003(d).

(3) The Issue of the Interferer's Privilege

Limitations, proportionate responsibility (Tex. Civ. Prac. & Rem. Code Ann. § 33.001 (Vernon 2004)), mitigation, inability to perform, and estoppel are available defenses in a tortious interference with existing contract action. *Hill*, 964 S.W.2d at 116 (limitations); *Sorbus, Inc. v. UHW Corp.*, 855 S.W.2d 771, 775 (Tex. App.—El Paso 1993, writ denied) (mitigation and inability to perform); *Frost Nat'l Bank v. Alamo Nat'l Bank*, 421 S.W.2d 153, 158 (Tex. App.—San Antonio 1967, writ ref'd n.r.e.) (estoppel). However, the most developed defenses under the case law are the defenses of privilege and justification. An issue in each tortious interference case is whether the defendant's actions were privileged or justified. Under the defense of legal justification or excuse, one is privileged to interfere with another's contractual relations if: (1) it is done in a bona fide exercise of his own rights or (2) he has an equal or superior right in the subject matter to that of the other party. *Victoria Bank & Trust Co.,* 811 S.W.2d at 939. If the defendant is legally excused in interfering with the contract, he is not liable to the plaintiff for the interference. *Marcus, Stowell & Beye Gov't Sec., Inc. v. Jefferson Inv. Corp.,* 797 F.2d 227, 235 (5th Cir. 1986).

Until 1989, Texas courts were split on whether the lack of justifiable privilege or legal excuse was an element of the plaintiff's cause of action for tortious interference, or whether privilege was an affirmative defense, to be pled and proved by the defendant. *Compare White v. Larson,* 586 S.W.2d 212, 215 (Tex. Civ. App.—El Paso 1979, no writ) (holding that a necessary element of a *prima facie* case for wrongful interference with a contract is that the acts of interference must have been done "without right or justifiable cause on the part of the defendant") *with Armendariz v. Mora,* 553 S.W.2d 400, 405 (Tex. Civ. App.—El Paso 1977, writ ref'd n.r.e.) (holding that the defendant has the burden to plead and prove privilege). Even the Texas Supreme Court was divided on the issue in its decision in *Sakowitz, Inc. v. Steck,* 669 S.W.2d 105 (Tex. 1984). The majority of the Court there decided that lack of justification or excuse should be viewed as an element of the plaintiff's right of recovery. *Id.* at 107. The dissent viewed justification or privilege as an affirmative defense. *Id.* at 108-09.

In *Sterner v. Marathon Oil Co.,* the Texas Supreme Court reversed prior decisions, holding that privilege to interfere with a contract is an affirmative defense on which the defendant has the burden of proof. 767 S.W.2d 686, 690 (Tex. 1989). The court reasoned that the party asserting legal justification or excuse does not deny the interference but rather seeks to avoid liability based upon a claimed interest that is being impaired or destroyed by the plaintiff's contract. *Id.* at 689-90; see also *Hill*, 964 S.W.2d at 124 (a defendant who has a superior financial interest is privileged to interfere with the contract of one who has an inferior financial interest).

Thus, under the defense of legal justification or excuse, one is privileged to interfere with another's contract if: (1) the interference is done in a bona fide exercise of the interferer's own rights, or (2) the party has equal or superior rights in the subject matter to that of the other party. *Sterner*, 767 S.W.2d at 691; see also *Murray v. Crest Constr., Inc.,* 900 S.W.2d 342, 344-45 (Tex. 1995); *Hopkins v. Highlands Ins. Co.,* 838 S.W.2d 819, 824 (Tex. App.—El Paso 1992, no writ); see also *Deauville Corp.*, 756 F.2d at 1198 (finding that the parent company's stock ownership in a subsidiary represents a financial interest superior to that of the other party's interest in the business relationship with the subsidiary and is privileged). Justification can be an affirmative defense to tortious interference with a contract based on a claim of one's own legal rights, even if that claim is ultimately proven to be a mistake. *Prudential Ins. Co. v. Fin. Review Servs., Inc.,* 29 S.W.3d 74, 80 (Tex. 2000); *Texas Beef Cattle Co. v. Green*, 921 S.W.2d 203, 211 (Tex. 1996).

The Texas Supreme Court has clarified that lack of good faith or the presence of common-law malice is

balancing agreements with oil well operators, by inform-
ing the operators that it would not take gas in accordance
with the operators' allocation until the working interest
owners agreed to settle claims against the pipeline
company. *Am. Nat. Petroleum Co. v. Transcon Gas Pipe
Line Corp.*, 798 S.W.2d 274, 278 (Tex. 1990).

C. Tortious Interference with Prospective Business Relations

The common law has long recognized that the
reasonable expectancy of a prospective contract or
business relationship is a property right that should
be protected from wrongful interference. *Leonard
Duckworth, Inc. v. Michael L. Field & Co.*, 516 F.2d 952,
955 (5th Cir. 1975). Texas law recognizes the cause of
action for tortious interference with prospective business
relations. However, authorities over the last few years
have substantially limited the scope of the claim.

(1) Wal-Mart Stores, Inc. v. Sturges

The Texas Supreme Court examined tortious
interference with prospective business relations
in *Wal-Mart Stores, Inc. v. Sturges*, 52 S.W.3d 711
(Tex. 2001). The court in *Sturges* established a new
standard by restricting the recovery in interference with
prospective business relations cases to situations where
the defendant's conduct was independently tortious or
otherwise unlawful.

Before the court's decision in *Sturges*, a plaintiff
had to satisfy the following four elements to recover in a

prospective relations claim: (1) a reasonable probability that the plaintiff would have entered into a contractual relationship; (2) the defendant acted maliciously by intentionally preventing the relationship from occurring, with the purpose of harming the plaintiff; (3) a lack of legal justification or excuse for the defendant's actions; and (4) actual harm or damage occurred as a result. *Milam v. Nat'l Ins. Crime Bureau,* 989 S.W.2d 126, 131 (Tex. App.—San Antonio 1999, no pet.).

Acknowledging a need to promote free competition, the Texas Supreme Court in *Sturges* rejected the malicious and intentional element, requiring instead that the plaintiff prove the defendant's conduct, aside from the interference, was either independently tortious or otherwise unlawful. *Id.* "Independently tortious" does not mean that a plaintiff must prove an independent tort; rather, the plaintiff must be able to demonstrate that the defendant's behavior would be actionable under a recognized tort. *Id.* Conduct that is simply sharp or "unfair" is not actionable and cannot serve as the basis for a claim of tortious interference with prospective business. *Id.*

(2) Definition and Elements

In the wake of the *Sturges* opinion, the Dallas, Eastland, San Antonio, Corpus Christi, Houston, and Waco Courts of Appeals have restated the elements of tortious interference with prospective business relations as: (1) a reasonable probability that the parties would have entered into a contractual relationship; (2) an independently tortious or unlawful act by the defendant that prevented the relationship from occurring; (3) the

The damages recoverable for tortious interference with business relations, both existing and prospective, are similar to those recoverable for tortious interference with a contract. A plaintiff may recover such damages sustained by him as are a natural and proximate consequence of the interference. *Gonzalez v. Gutierrez,* 694 S.W.2d 384, 390 (Tex. App.—San Antonio 1985, no writ). A plaintiff may recover: (1) the pecuniary loss of the benefits of the contract or the prospective relation; (2) consequential losses for which the interference is a legal cause; and (3) emotional distress or actual harm to reputation if they are reasonably to be expected to result from the interference. *Id.* (quoting RESTATEMENT (SECOND) OF TORTS § 774A (1979)).

(e) Mental Anguish Damages

If a plaintiff establishes an intentional tort, mental anguish damages are available as an element of actual damage. *Harned v. E-Z Fin. Co.,* 254 S.W.2d 81, 85 (Tex. 1953). Therefore, mental anguish damages are an available element of damages for tortious interference with existing or prospective contracts. *Exxon Corp.,* 808 S.W.2d at 660; *Comstock Silversmiths, Inc. v. Carey,* 894 S.W.2d 56, 58 n.2 (Tex. App.—San Antonio 1995, no writ).

(f) Exemplary Damages

Exemplary damages are available in suits involving claims for tortious interference with prospective contracts. *Bard v. Charles R. Myers Ins. Agency, Inc.,* 811 S.W.2d 251, 263 (Tex. App.— San Antonio 1991), *rev'd on other grounds,* 839 S.W.2d 791 (Tex. 1992). To recover exemplary damages in this context, the plaintiff must show that the defendant acted with malice. *Id.* As with a claim for tortious interference with an existing contract the liability, actual malice, damages, and the amount of exemplary damages must be unanimous.

(3) Examples

Since *Sturges*, there do not appear to have been any authorities affirming a claim of tortious interference with a prospective relationship or contract. However, cases have declined to find tortious interference with prospective relations. For example, a temporary injunction issued seeking to prohibit competition for a prospective business relationship was reversed because plaintiffs failed to show that the defendant engaged in independently tortious or unlawful acts. *Allied Capital Corp. v. Cravens,* 67 S.W.3d 486 (Tex. App.—Corpus Christi 2002, no pet.).

D. Interference with Contract and Interference with Prospective Relations Compared

In suits for interference with a contract, the defendant's willful interference with a contract is actionable, as opposed to a suit for interference with prospective business relations where a plaintiff must show that, in addition to willfully interfering with business relations, the defendant's conduct was otherwise unlawful or independently tortious. This difference makes an action for interference with prospective business relations more difficult to prove. Further, unlike cases of interference with a contract, in actions for interference with prospective business relations, justification and privilege are not available as affirmative defenses, except to the extent they may be defenses to the underlying allegedly tortious or unlawful conduct. *Sturges*, 52 S.W.3d at 726-27.

IX. UNFAIR COMPETITION (INCLUDING MISAPPROPRIATION, TRADEMARKS, TRADE DRESS, AND TRADE NAMES)

A. Introduction

B. Misappropriation

C. Trademarks, Trade Dress, and Trade Names

   (1) Differentiation

      (a) Trade Marks

      (b) Trade Name

      (c) Trade Dress

   (2) Acquisition of Rights

   (3) Levels of Protection Available

      (a) Common Law

      (b) State Registration

      (c) Federal Registration

   (4) Loss of Rights

      (a) Section 43(a) of the Lanham Act (15 U.S.C. § 1125(a) (1993))

   (5) Enforcement

      (a) Elements

A. Introduction

Unfair competition is a broad type of business tort, covering many of the topics discussed in this paper. "The law of unfair competition is the umbrella for all statutory and nonstatutory causes of action arising out of business conduct which is contrary to honest practice in industrial or commercial matters." *Taylor Publ'g Co. v. Jostens, Inc.*, 216 F.3d 465, 486 (5th Cir. 2000) (*quoting American Heritage Life Ins. Co. v. Heritage Life Ins. Co.*, 494 F.2d 3, 14 (5th Cir. 1974)); 3 R. Callman, The Law of Unfair Competition § 4.1, at 120 (3d ed.1969). Within the broad scope of unfair competition are the independent causes of action such as trade secret law, "palming off" or "passing off," and misappropriation, to name only a few. W. Page Keeton et al., Prosser and Keeton on the Law of Torts § 130 at 1013-30 (5th ed. 1984). Myriad activities can constitute unfair competition. The basic tenet is that the plaintiff has a property right in the public's recognition of a particular good or service, and any conduct by another that undermines the value of that property right is subject to scrutiny. Courts are more aggressive in enjoining such conduct and, upon proof of actual confusion, will award the plaintiff monetary relief for his damages.

B. Misappropriation

Misappropriation is classified as a type of unfair competition but is more akin to the tort of theft of trade secrets (or misappropriation of confidential information). This tort has been discussed by relatively few Texas courts and has not been specifically recognized by the Texas Supreme Court, but it has received increasing recognition in the last several years.

"The doctrine of misappropriation is a branch of the tort of unfair competition which involves the appropriation and use by the defendant, in competition with the plaintiff, of a unique pecuniary interest created by the plaintiff through the expenditure of labor, skill and money. It is recognized under Texas law." *Universal City Studios v. Kamar Indus.,* 217 U.S.P.Q. 1162, 1168 (S.D. Tex. 1982) (citations omitted) (approved in *R. Ready Prods., Inc. v. Cantrell,* 85 F. Supp.2d 672 (S.D. Tex. 2000)).

As explained in *Gilmore v. Sammons,* 269 S.W. 861, 863 (Tex. Civ. App.—Dallas 1925, writ ref'd), the original basis for the tort of misappropriation is rooted in federal common law, including a case involving misappropriation

337 n.1 (5th Cir. 1984) (observing that "'[t]rade dress' is a concept which embraces the total image of a given product, including advertising materials and marketing techniques used to promote its sale"). Under appropriate circumstances, aspects of trade dress may be registrable under the Lanham Act and under the Texas trademark statute.

Even if distinctive, not all trade dress is protectable. To be protectable, trade dress must be "non-functional." A functional feature is one "which is essential to the use or purpose of the article or [that] affects the cost or quality of the article." *Inwood Labs., Inc. v. Ives Labs., Inc.*, 456 U.S. 844, 850 n.10 (1982). Functional features are not protectable under trade dress law because of the reluctance of courts to extend potentially perpetual, patent-like protection to a product or feature that may not qualify for patent protection. *Traffix Devices, Inc. v. Mktg. Displays, Inc.*, 532 U.S. 23, 30 (2001) (ruling that a dual spring mechanism allowing signs to withstand strong winds was functional and not entitled to trade dress protection). This reluctance is well founded because to allow protection of functional features would foreclose competition. For example, the unique shape of a Coke bottle is protectable, but not the concept of a glass container with a small hole for consumption using the same functions. The characteristics that are protectable are non-functional and, therefore, do not foreclose competition.

(2) Acquisition of Rights

In the United States, rights in a mark, trade name, or trade dress are acquired by adoption and use.

Although one or both may be advisable, federal and state registrations are not required.

All marks, however, are not created equal. Some marks will be entitled to broader protection than others and some marks will be entitled to protection immediately upon adoption and use, while other marks must be used for some time before any rights will be developed. Finally, some terms may never be protectable regardless of the length and extent of use. As the four categories listed below illustrate, the difference in treatment depends upon the relationship of the mark to the goods or services provided under the mark:

(1) "Arbitrary or fanciful" marks are terms or phrases which are either coined phrases or words that are not suggestive of the product or service (e.g., Kodak for cameras and film);

(2) "Suggestive" terms or phrases suggest rather than describe some characteristic of the product or service (e.g., Roach Motel for insect traps);

(3) "Descriptive" terms identify a characteristic or quality of the product or service (e.g., Steak & Brew for restaurant services). Geographic terms and personal names are treated as descriptive; and

(4) "Generic" terms or phrases identify a genus or class of products or services (e.g., Shredded Wheat for baked wheat biscuits).

See, e.g., *Union Nat'l Bank of Tex., Laredo v. Union Nat'l Bank of Tex., Austin*, 909 F.2d 839, 845 (5th Cir. 1990).

Marks, trade names, and trade dress that are arbitrary, fanciful, or suggestive are "inherently distinctive" and are protectable immediately upon adoption and use. In contrast, marks, trade names, and trade dress that are descriptive or otherwise not inherently distinctive are only protectable after sufficient use has been made to demonstrate "secondary meaning" as discussed below. See, e.g., *Two Pesos*, 23 U.S.P.Q.2d 1081; *Union Nat'l Bank*, 909 F.2d at 844; *Zapata Corp. v. Zapata Trading Int'l, Inc.*, 841 S.W.2d 45, 47 (Tex. App.—Houston [14th Dist.] 1992, no writ).

Marks fall at various locations along this spectrum; in close cases, it is difficult, if not impossible, to predict how a court might categorize a particular mark. The correct categorization of a given term is a question of fact, and this initial determination is of crucial importance because secondary meaning can be difficult and costly to establish. *Union Nat'l Bank*, 909 F.2d at 846.

(3) Levels of Protection Available

Trademarks, trade dress, and trade names are protected by overlapping causes of action arising under federal statutory law, state statutory law, and state common law. Due in large part to an ever-expanding application of one section of the federal trademark statute, 15 U.S.C. § 1125(a) (section 43(a) of the Lanham Act), the differences between federal, state, and common-law protections are rapidly disappearing. Today, virtually any cause of action for trademark, trade dress, or trade name infringement or unfair competition, in general, may be brought in federal court pursuant to section 43(a) of the Lanham Act, regardless of whether a federally registered mark is involved.

(a) Common Law

Common-law rights are acquired through use. The scope of common-law protection is limited to the geographic area of the actual use. Regardless of the existence of registrations, priority of use, not priority of registration, generally determines superiority of rights in marks. Obtaining federal or state registrations do, however, provide procedural and evidentiary advantages.

(b) State Registration

Rights are acquired through use and registration under state statutes. Rights vary from state to state depending upon statute, but many provide for statewide protection regardless of the geographic area of use. Texas has enacted a trademark statute. Tex. Bus. & Comm. Code Ann. §§ 16.01-.28 (Vernon 1987 and Vernon Supp. 1993).

(c) Federal Registration

Federal rights are acquired through both use and registration. Benefits of federal registration include nationwide constructive use and notice provisions as well as the possibility of acquiring "incontestable" status. Nationwide constructive use and notice provisions protect the right to expand nationwide. 15 U.S.C. § 1057(c) (1993). "Incontestable" status is available for federally registered marks after five years from the date of registration and severely restricts defenses which may be raised in an action for infringement of the registered mark. 15 U.S.C. §§ 1065, 1115(l) (1993).

(4) Loss of Rights

Trademarks, trade names, and trade dress are relatively fragile property rights that can easily be forfeited. Intentional abandonment occurs when one discontinues use of a mark with an express or implied intent to abandon the mark. With federal registrations, non-use for a two-year period gives rise to a presumption that the owner intended to abandon the registration. 15 U.S.C. § 1127 (1993); *Exxon Corp. v. Humble Exploration Co.*, 695 F.2d 96 (5th Cir. 1983).

"Unintentional" or "technical" abandonment may occur while the mark is being used and without an intent to abandon the mark. Unintentional or technical abandonment arises from acts of commission or omission that cause a mark to lose its distinctiveness or its significance as a source indicator. Situations that may lead to unintentional or technical abandonment include: uncontrolled licensing (lack of adequate quality control); assignment of a mark "in gross" or without the accompanying good will (for example, purchasing a mark for use in connection with dissimilar goods or services or for use in connection with goods or services of significantly different quality); or widespread improper use of the trademark as the generic term for the goods or services (e.g., "Escalator" and "Aspirin" were originally trademarks but became the generic names for moving stairs and pain relievers, respectively).

(a) Section 43(a) of the Lanham Act (15 U.S.C. § 1125(a) (1993))

Section 43(a) of the Lanham Act warrants special attention because the umbrella of conduct covered by this section continues to expand. The broad language of section 43(a) provides federal jurisdiction for a wide variety of tortious conduct such as trademark, trade name, trade dress infringement, unfair competition (regardless of whether a federally registered mark is involved), false advertising, and violations of individuals' rights of publicity. This section is occasionally referred to as the "federal unfair competition statute." The section is quoted in section II(c)(1) supra.

Sub-paragraph (a)(1) frequently provides federal jurisdiction in cases involving unregistered trademarks, trade names, trade dress, etc. Sub-paragraph (a)(2) provides federal jurisdiction in cases involving false advertising or product disparagement. As discussed below, the full range of remedies available in federal trademark infringement actions is available in actions brought under section 43(a) of the Lanham Act.

(5) Enforcement

(a) Elements

The issues of federal trademark infringement, state trademark infringement, and common-law trademark infringement, as well as infringement of trade names and trade dress and unfair competition, all involve generally the same inquiry and require the same elements of proof:

(1) plaintiff has a protectable interest in the trademark, trade name, or trade dress;

(2) plaintiff is a senior (earlier) user of the trademark, trade name, or trade dress;

(3)   there is a likelihood of confusion between the plaintiff's trademark, trade name, or trade dress and that of the other user; and

(4)   to obtain injunctive relief, the plaintiff must show that the likelihood of confusion will cause irreparable injury.

See, e.g., *Two Pesos*, 23 U.S.P.Q.2d 1081; *Union Nat'l*, 909 F.2d 839 at 844; *Interstate Battery Sys. of Am., Inc. v. Wright*, 811 F.Supp. 237 (N.D. Tex. 1993); *Zapata*, 841 S.W.2d at 47.

(b) Protectable Interest

To establish a protectable interest in a trademark, trade name, or trade dress, a plaintiff must establish use of a trademark, trade name, or trade dress that is inherently distinctive (°e., arbitrary, fanciful, or sugges-tive) or that has acquired distinctiveness or secondary meaning.   See, e.g., *Two Pesos*, 23 U.S.P.Q.2d 1081; *Wal-Mart Stores, Inc. v. Samara Brothers, Inc.*, 529 U.S. 205 (2000) (product design, like color, not distinctive); *Union Nat'l Bank*, 909 F.2d at 844; *Zapata*, 841 S.W.2d at 47-48.

"'Secondary meaning' is a term of art in trade-mark law. It refers to the situation that arises when a person has a mark that might ordinarily be ineligible for protection were it not for the fact that the name has come to be closely associated (in a distinct market) with a particular manufacturer's product or service." *Union Nat'l Bank*, 909 F.2d at 841 n.3.

"This is a substantial burden and it must be shown [that] the name or mark denotes to the consumer a single thing coming from a single source. Both direct and circumstantial evidence may be used to establish secondary meaning. Evidence such as amount and manner of advertising, volume of sales, and length and manner of use may constitute circumstantial evidence relevant to the issue of secondary meaning. These factors combined may prove secondary meaning; together they can establish the necessary link in the minds of consumers between the product and source." *Zapata*, 841 S.W.2d at 48.

(c) Likelihood of Confusion

Likelihood of confusion is a question of fact. See, e.g., *Moore Bus. Forms, Inc. v. Ryu*, 960 F.2d 486, 489 (5th Cir. 1992); *Interstate Battery*, 811 F. Supp. at 241. The confusion may be as to source or origin, affiliation, connection, or sponsorship. A number of factors are considered in determining the likelihood of confusion element:

> The type of trademark at issue, that is, the strength of the trademark; degree of similarity between the two marks; similarity of products; identity of retail outlets and purchasers; identity of advertising media utilized; defendant's intent; and actual confusion.

Moore Bus. Forms, 960 F.2d at 489-90; *Interstate Battery*, 811 F. Supp. at 241; *Zapata*, 841 S.W.2d at 49. None of these factors is dispositive, and different factors will weigh more heavily from case to case. *Moore Bus. Forms*, 960 F.2d at 490. Actual confusion, although not required, is typically the strongest evidence of a likelihood of confusion. *Id.* at 491; *Zapata*, 841 S.W.2d at 49. In *Associated Telephone*, the plaintiff at trial used the testimony of three actual customers to show confusion over the sponsorship of the "Heart of the Hills" directory. 849 S.W.2d 894

(6) Remedies

(a) Injunctive Relief

Injunctive relief is provided for by both the Lanham Act and the Texas trademark statute and is the form of relief that courts prefer in infringement actions. 15 U.S.C. § 1116 (1993); Tex. Bus. & Comm. Code § 16.26(c) (Vernon 1987). A full range of injunctive relief is available, from *ex parte* seizure orders in egregious cases such as counterfeiting, to temporary restraining orders, preliminary injunctions, and permanent injunctions. See, e.g., *Texas Pig Stands, Inc. v. Hard Rock Cafe Int'l, Inc.*, 951 F.2d 684 (5th Cir.); *Roho, Inc. v. Marquis*, 902 F.2d 356 (5th Cir. 1990); *Better Bus. Bureau of Metro. Houston, Inc. v. Med. Dir., Inc.*, 681 F.2d 397 (5th Cir. 1982); *Interstate Battery*, 811 F.Supp. at 245.

(b) Monetary Relief

"Subject to the principles of equity," a plaintiff may recover the defendant's profits, the plaintiff's damages, and costs of an action. 15 U.S.C. § 1117(a) (1993); Tex. Bus. & Comm. Code § 16.26(c) (Vernon 1987). In "exceptional cases," a party may recover attorneys' fees. 15 U.S.C. § 1117. Under the Lanham Act, the amount awarded may also be enhanced as provided in 15 U.S.C. § 1117.

Monetary relief is the exception rather than the rule in trademark, trade name, and trade dress infringement actions, and it is difficult to obtain absent proof of actual confusion or clear proof of lost sales. Most jurisdictions will allow recovery of monetary relief to deter a willful infringer. See, e.g., *Getty Petroleum Corp. v. Bartco Petroleum Corp.*, 858 F.2d 103, 113 (2d Cir. 1988). However, the Fifth Circuit appears to require more than a showing of willful infringement before awarding monetary relief. *Texas Pig Stands,* 951 F.2d at 698-699.

Similarly, the requirement of exceptional circumstances for the recovery of attorney's fees is typically "interpreted by courts to require a showing of a high degree of culpability on the part of the infringer, for example, bad faith or fraud." *Moore Bus. Forms*, 960 F.2d at 492; see also *CJC Holdings, Inc. v. Wright & Lato, Inc.*, 979 F.2d 60 (5th Cir. 1992), *rev'd on other grounds*, 989 F.2d 791 (1993); *Interstate Battery*, 811 F.Supp. at 246.

(c) Defendant's Profits for Damages for Trademark Infringement

In assessing profits, the plaintiff is required to prove defendant's sales only. 15 U.S.C. § 1117(a). Defendant must prove all elements of cost or deduction claimed. *Id.* There are six factors that courts consider in determining whether an award of profits is appropriate: (1) whether the defendant had the intent to confuse or deceive; (2) whether sales had been diverted; (3) the adequacy of other remedies; (4) any unreasonable delay by the plaintiff in asserting his rights; (5) the public interest in making the misconduct unprofitable; and (6) whether it is a case of palming off. *Seatrax, Inc.*

v. Sonbeck Intern., Inc., 200 F.3d 358, 369 (5th Cir. 2000) (noting that an award of the defendant's profit is not automatic).

(d) Plaintiff's Actual Damages for Trademark Infringement

The plaintiff can recover damages for all injuries caused by the infringer's wrongful act regardless of whether the infringer anticipated or contemplated the injuries. *Hamilton Brown Shoe Co. v. Wolf Bros. & Co.,* 240 U.S. 251, 259 (1916). The courts have allowed plaintiffs to recover for a wide variety of damages. See, e.g., *Taco Cabana,* 932 F.2d at 1125 (accepting plaintiff's "headstart" theory of damages incurred in markets of plaintiff's logical area of expansion thereby precluding plaintiff from receiving profits and licensing fees that it otherwise would have realized).

The courts seem to be split on the award of corrective advertising. *Compare U-Haul Int'l, Inc. v. Jartran, Inc.,* 793 F.2d 1034, 1041 (9th Cir. 1986) (permitting award of corrective advertising even though the amount spent by plaintiff was more than double the amount of the original false advertising by the defendant) *with Zazu Designs v. Loreal S.A.,* 979 F.2d 499, 506 (7th Cir. 1992) (criticizing the corrective advertising theory of recovery by analogizing trademark damages to vehicle damage).

The Fifth Circuit has held that royalties normally received for the use of a mark are the proper measure of damages for misuse of those marks. *Boston Prof'l Hockey Ass'n, Inc. v. Dallas Cap & Emblem Mfg., Inc.,* 597 F.2d 71, 76 (5th Cir. 1979).

(e) Enhanced Damages for Trademark Infringement

15 U.S.C. § 1117(a) also gives the court discretionary power to increase damages for any sum above the amount found as actual damages, not exceeding three times such amount. In addition, the court has the discretion to increase or decrease an award based on profits if the award is either inadequate or excessive. Courts have engrafted a willful prerequisite in forcing the defendant to account for his profits, and they have also required a finding of willful infringement before damages will be enhanced. *Rolex Watch USA, Inc. v. Meece,* 158 F.3d 816, 826 (5th Cir. 1998), *cert. denied,* 526 U.S. 1133 (1999). The Fifth Circuit has also taken the position that increased damages may be justified in cases where the defendant withholds or misrepresents its sales records. *Boston Prof'l Hockey Ass'n,* 597 F.2d at 77.

(7) Related Protection - Dilution

"Dilution" is the gradual diminution or whittling away of the distinctive quality of a famous mark caused by third party uses, regardless of any likelihood of confusion. For example, the famous Tiffany mark for a New York jeweler may be diluted by use of the Tiffany mark for restaurants, even though there may be no likelihood of confusion due to the dissimilarities of the services offered under the marks.

In 1996, Congress amended the Lanham Act to include a federal anti-dilution statute patterned after state statutes to protect famous trademarks. 15 U.S.C. § 1125(c). Over half of the states have anti-dilution statutes. The Texas anti-dilution statute provides:

[a] person may bring an action to enjoin an act likely to injure a business reputation or to dilute the distinctive quality of a mark registered under this chapter or Title 15, U.S.C., or a mark or trade name valid at common law, regardless of whether there is competition between the parties or confusion as to the source of goods or services. An injunction sought under this section shall be obtained pursuant to Rule 680 *et seq.* of the Texas Rules of Civil Procedure.

Tex. Bus. & Comm. Code Ann. § 16.29 (Vernon Supp. 1993). Note that the statute provides for only injunctive relief.

Case law applying the Texas statute is sparse. Few reported cases mention the statute, and only one applies the statute and finds the defendant guilty of dilution (without any discussion of the finding). See, e.g., *CJC Holdings,* 979 F.2d 60 (statute asserted but not discussed); *National Football League Prop. v. Playoff Corp.,* 808 F. Supp. 1288 (N.D. Tex. 1992) (statute cited but not applied); *Serv. Merch. Co. v. Serv. Jewelry Stores, Inc.,* 737 F. Supp. 983, 990 (S.D. Tex. 1990) (dilution found without discussion).

It is likely that in applying the Texas dilution statute, Texas courts will look to the application of similar state statutes in other jurisdictions, such as applications of New York's dilution statute, N.Y. Gen. Bus. Law § 368-d. Courts have typically disfavored anti-dilution statutes and have narrowly construed them. A major limitation that many courts have read into these anti-dilution statutes is a requirement that a mark be "famous" before it qualifies for protection against dilution. See, e.g., *Mead Data Cent., Inc. v. Toyota Motor Sales, Inc.*, 875 F.2d 1026 (2d Cir. 1989) ("LEXIS" mark for computerized legal services was not yet widely enough known to be diluted by "LEXUS" mark for automobiles).

There is a two-year statute of limitations for unfair competition claims. Tex. Bus. & Comm. Code Ann. § 16.003; see also *Derrick Mfg. Corp. v. Southwestern Wire Cloth, Inc.*, 934 F.Supp. 796, 806 (S.D. Tex. 1996).